THE M & E HANDBOOK SERIES

Elements of Banking

D. P. Whiting
MTech, BSc (Econ), AIB, MInstAM

THIRD EDITION

MACDONALD AND EVANS

85653316

Macdonald and Evans Ltd.
Estover, Plymouth PL6 7PZ

First published 1975
Reprinted 1976 (twice)
Reprinted 1978
Second Edition 1979
Reprinted 1982
Third Edition 1985

© Macdonald & Evans Ltd 1985

British Library Cataloguing in Publication Data

Whiting, D.P.
    Elements of banking.——3rd ed.——(The
M & E handbook series)
    1. Banks and banking——Great Britain
    I. Title
    332.1′0941   HG2988

    ISBN 0-7121-0657-X

332.1

Printed in Great Britain by
J. W. ARROWSMITH LIMITED
Winterstoke Road
Bristol BS3 2NT

Preface to the Third Edition

The British banking system has changed dramatically during the last twenty years, both in its role as an intricate part of the monetary system controlled by the Government and in its services to its customers. This book provides a basic knowledge of this monetary and financial system and the place of the banks within the national economy. The framework within which the banks conduct their operations is considered in detail, together with the range of services which they provide to both personal and business customers.

Thus the reader with a desire to have a general knowledge of the banking system will find his wants satisfied by this book but, primarily, it is intended for the banking student following a BTEC National Certificate (or Diploma) Course or a Banker's Conversion Course as his first step to becoming an Associate of the Institute of Bankers. The subject, Elements of Banking, provides a good base for the specialised Banking subjects in Stage II of the Banking Diploma Examinations, i.e. Law Relating to Banking, Accountancy, Finance of International Trade, Monetary Economics and Practice of Banking. All of these subjects will fall more readily into place if the student has first gained a sound knowledge of the Elements of Banking.

This third edition meets the Learning Objectives of the Business and Technician Education Council's (BTEC) option modules *Elements of Banking I & II*. Additional chapters have been included and other revisions made, to ensure that these objectives are fully covered and the data has been updated.

Method of study. The student is advised to work through each part of the book in strict sequence. Read quickly through the notes to get the broad picture of the contents and then, on reading a second time, do so in more detail, making sure that you understand each paragraph before passing on to the next. The student should then read the notes a third time and memorise the essential facts.

Progress tests. These tests are meant for self-examination. They are placed at the end of each chapter and should not be attempted until the chapter has been thoroughly learnt. Try to answer each question in full and then check your answer with the text (by means of the chapter and paragraph references printed after each question). Make frequent use of these tests, as they are the best way of memorising the subject.

Test papers and examination technique. Appendixes of test papers and hints on examination technique are to be found at the end of the book. Do not attempt any of the test papers until you have mastered the hints on examination technique and have achieved complete confidence in answering the Progress Tests at the end of the relevant chapters.

When you attempt a test paper, do it under strict examination conditions and mark yourself by checking with the section references to the appropriate part of the text.

1985   DPW

Contents

Table of Cases

Table of Statutes

PART ONE

MONEY AND CREDIT

CHAPTER I

The Origins and Functions of Money

HISTORY OF MONEY

1. Specialisation and exchange. When originally man was self-sufficient, in that he provided all the basic needs, food, clothing and shelter, for himself and his family through such activities as hunting and fishing, there was no need for money.

As soon as specialisation took place, however, goods had to be exchanged one for another and this raised the problem of the rate of exchange and suggested the possible need for some form of medium of exchange. The man who was good at fishing concentrated on that activity and left the good huntsmen to do the hunting. In this way both benefited, as the total yield of both fish and meat was likely to be more than if they had both fished and hunted.

2. Barter. The exchange of one commodity directly for another, e.g. fish for n.eat, is called barter. Whereas this system of direct exchange is possible within a small community in which the pattern of trade is a simple one, it is hardly conceivable in a modern society. In fact we would not have our present highly complex economy if alternatives to barter had not been found.

Barter raises many problems which are easy to imagine and which do not need to be dwelt upon in answers to examination questions. A brief list of them will suffice!

(*a*) The rate of exchange – how is it to be measured?

(*b*) Large indivisible units – a live animal, for instance, cannot be divided into small units to exchange for other small items.

(*c*) Consistent quality.

(*d*) Perishable commodities.

(*e*) Transport and storage of commodities in order to exchange them.

3. Indirect exchange. Because of the difficulties of the barter system, one or more commodities prized above others, because they were scarce or particularly useful, became the medium of exchange. These were commodities that were readily acceptable as a means of payment for goods. For example shells, oxen, salt, spears, amber, cotton cloth and bags of grain have at times been used in this way. They were in fact the original forms of money in that they were a medium of exchange and a unit of account.

4. Precious metals. The commodities originally used as money tended to be bulky, not very durable, and not consistent in quality. In fact they had many of the disadvantages of barter. Metals such as bronze, copper, gold and silver, on the other hand, were valuable and hence only relatively small quantities were required to settle transactions. They therefore became popular as money. Furthermore, they could be weighed and marked with their weights and from this came the introduction of coins. Many of the present-day coins owe their names to the weights used in those times, e.g. the pound and the pennyweight.

FUNCTIONS OF MONEY

5. Medium of exchange. From what has been considered so far it is clear that the most obvious function of money is to act as a medium of exchange. It permits indirect exchange, but for this the money must be relatively scarce and readily acceptable by those who have goods or services to sell. To be acceptable it must be reasonably stable in value so that the holder knows that he will be able to obtain roughly the same quantity of goods and services with it when he chooses to spend it.

6. A unit of account. In addition to being a medium of exchange, money must be a unit of account. It must be a measuring rod by which the values of all other commodities can be assessed. Instead of measuring the value of a commodity in terms of other commodities, as it is necessary to do in a system of barter, each unit of a commodity is valued in terms of the unit of money. Not only does money enable goods to be indirectly exchanged, but also the value of output can be measured and recorded in money terms. Our gross national product can be quoted as so many thousands of millions of pounds, instead of so many cars plus so many ships, and so on.

7. A standard for deferred payments. Primarily, money can be said to have two functions, a medium of exchange and a unit of account, but in addition it is desirable that it should be a standard for deferred payments. In other words, it is a means whereby debts may be measured and recorded and without which all transactions would have to be for cash and there would be no need for the banks and other financial institutions. This implies that money is a store of value, which is the next and last basic function of money.

8. A store of value. The value of money must remain relatively constant, otherwise people would not wish to hold it. This is what is meant by a store of value. Even during the recent periods of rather severe inflation, however, when the value of money has fallen quite rapidly, it has continued to function as money. But there is a limit beyond which confidence in a currency drops so much that the holders of it will switch to commodities as soon as possible. When such a situation gets out of hand, a country is said to have hyper-inflation and the consequence is certain to be that the money supply will have to be replaced. This happened in Germany in 1922–3 and in Hungary after the Second World War. Until a new form of money is issued, the community will devise its own form of money by using such things as cigarettes as the medium of exchange and unit of account.

9. Money and the price mechanism. In a free society money, through the price mechanism, determines the allocation of goods and services. Apart from the limited number of goods which are controlled by the state, e.g. drugs and firearms for which some form of authority or licence must be obtained, the price mechanism and our willingness and ability to pay the price determines who is going to have the goods or services. At the other extreme, in a completely totalitarian state, all the goods and services are produced and distributed by the state and it is just conceivable that the community could manage without money, though this would not be very practical in our modern world.

Through its four functions, money thus plays a vital role in the community.

PROGRESS TEST 1

1. What is meant by specialisation and exchange? **(1)**
2. Distinguish between barter and indirect exchange. **(2, 3)**

3. Why did the precious metals become used as money?   **(4)**

4. What is meant by a medium of exchange and a unit of account? **(5, 6)**

5. What is the connection between a standard for deferred payments and a store of value?   **(7, 8)**

6. Why is money so important in a free society?   **(9)**

CHAPTER II

Coins and Notes

THE COINAGE

1. The use of precious metals. In our present-day society coins represent only the small change in our money supply, but it is only seventy years or so ago that gold sovereigns freely circulated in Britain and gold and silver coins were the main form of currency in most countries. For many centuries the precious metals had been used to produce coins of recognisable shapes, sizes and denominations. Coins were acceptable as a medium of exchange because of these qualities and also because they had an intrinsic value, i.e. they had value in themselves as gold, silver, copper, etc. This intrinsic value was usually fixed by law.

2. The British coinage. The pound came into existence in Anglo-Saxon times as a unit of account when it was decreed that the pound of silver should be minted into 240 pennies. Until the end of the thirteenth century the penny was virtually the only coin in circulation in Britain. The word shilling was probably derived from the name of the piece of silver that was thrown into the scales to make up the weight when payment was made by weight of silver, and later became used to denote twelve pence.

The silver weight of the penny was 22.5 gr. troy when William the Conqueror established his main Mint at the Tower of London. Subsequently, baser coins were circulated from time to time which had a lower silver content, but the penny sterling was recognised on the Continent during William's reign for having a fairly consistent fineness of silver, and was readily accepted for commercial purposes. Some gold coins, particularly nobles (a third of a pound) were minted prior to the fifteenth century and gold and silver coins circulated side by side but it was not until 1489 that the first gold sovereign worth £1 was minted and five years later the first silver shilling piece was introduced.

3. Clipping and debasing the coinage. From Norman times until the eighteenth century unscrupulous people clipped, filed, washed and sweated coins and profited from the sale of the gold and silver thus derived. The most common of the practices was that of clipping pieces from the edges of the coins. Coins were often clipped down to nearly half their weight with the result that recoinages were frequently required. The remedy against clipping was the milled edge which was introduced in the seventeenth century.

The coinage was frequently debased, i.e. its official gold or silver content was reduced by the monarch in order to provide him with finance. By substituting more alloy for gold or silver when minting the precious metals into coins it was not difficult to make a profit.

4. The gold standard. Gold took over from silver as the standard for the British currency during the eighteenth century. Silver became worth more as a commodity than the mint price, mostly because the metal was greatly in demand in India and very few silver coins were minted during the century. Gold, on the other hand, was imported into Britain in very large quantities at this time and more gold coins were minted in the first half of the eighteenth century that in the previous century and a half.

The gold guinea was the standard coin for roughly a century prior to the general use of the sovereign after 1817. The Mint price of gold remained at £3.17s.10½d. (approx. £3.89) per standard ounce for most of the two hundred years up to 1914 and formed the basis of the international gold standard which existed until then and was temporarily resumed from 1925 until its final breakdown in 1931. Bank of England notes were convertible into gold from 1821 and remained so up to 1931, apart from three short periods of crisis when the Bank was released from its obligation to pay out in gold.

BANKING AND THE NOTE ISSUE

5. Bank-notes. In Biblical times the "bankers" were often the priests who could be trusted to take care of valuables, especially gold and silver, deposited with them. The temples were also the strongest, and hence the safest, buildings in which to store these assets.

In Britain our first bankers were the London goldsmiths who from the seventeenth century onwards flourished not only as craftsmen in gold and silver but as persons who would take deposits of gold and silver coins for safe-keeping. The goldsmiths made a profit by sorting the coins that were deposited with them, taking out the full-weight coins and exporting them. They gave receipts for the deposits which had to be presented to them when withdrawals were required. As the goldsmiths were well known and trusted, so too were the receipts that they issued, and they therefore tended to pass from hand to hand in settlement for debts. It was often more convenient to settle an account in this way than to have to visit the goldsmith, withdraw a deposit in coins and pass these coins on to the person who was to be paid. He in turn would have had to take the coins to the goldsmith and deposit them with him for safe-keeping.

The goldsmiths found it very convenient to have their receipts circulated in this way, especially as the process enabled them to lend money. They became aware that it was reasonable to assume that at any one time only a small percentage of the gold and silver deposited with them would be demanded back by the depositors, and that this percentage would become more and more reduced as depositors made increasing use of the receipts as a means of payment. The goldsmiths could then make loans and charge interest for the service, and this was a very rewarding occupation; so much so that the goldsmiths encouraged the circulation of their receipts by issuing them payable to bearer and in convenient denominations, e.g. £10 and £5. This was the origin of the bank-note.

6. Private note issues. The development of the commercial banking system and the dominance of the Bank of England as the central bank will be considered in detail in Part Three but it is necessary at this stage to trace the development of the note issues from those of the goldsmiths to that of the Bank of England today. Gradually the original bankers gave up their work as goldsmiths and concentrated on their more profitable activities, i.e. accepting deposits and lending money. They were joined by other types of merchants and industrialists, such as corn merchants and worsted weavers, who through their commercial activities had become well-known and trusted. Collectively, they formed a large group of private banks which flourished through to the nineteenth century as independent concerns with their own private note issues.

A series of Bank Acts in the nineteenth century, especially the Bank Charter Act 1844, brought a gradual end to the private note issues. As the private banks merged with the newly emerging joint-stock banks so their note-issuing powers became vested in the Bank of England. The last of the private note issues to disappear was that of Fox, Fowler and Company. This occurred when the bank was absorbed by Lloyds Bank in 1921. The Bank of England then had (and still has) a monopoly of the note issue in Britain, though some banks, especially in Scotland, have been permitted to continue to issue their own notes provided that they are backed pound for pound with Bank of England notes. The total of the Bank of England's note issue thus represents the total of notes issued in Britain. (The Scottish banks have a very limited fiduciary issue which is negligible in comparison with the Bank of England's note issue.)

THE CURRENT NOTE ISSUE

7. The fiduciary issue. An issue of bank-notes which is not backed by gold is said to be fiduciary, i.e. "issued in trust", and the Bank of England's present note issue (£11,500 million at the time of writing) is entirely fiduciary. This issue is backed by Government securities and not by gold, and its amount is controlled by HM Treasury within the provisions of the Currency and Bank Notes Act 1954.

The Bank Charter Act 1844 laid down that the Bank of England's fiduciary issue should be £14 million, and that this should be increased by two-thirds of the amount of the note issue of any private bank when the bank became merged with another bank or closed down. At the outset of the First World War the Treasury issued its own notes, and by 1919 the fiduciary issue had risen to £320 million. The Treasury's note issue was taken over by the Bank of England in 1928 and by virtue of the Currency and Bank Notes Act of that year the fiduciary issue was fixed at £260 million. The Act also provided that the Treasury could authorise the Bank of England to issue notes beyond this limit for a period not exceeding six months. A series of Currency and Bank Notes Acts since 1928 has gradually increased the size of the note issue. The Act of 1954 empowered the Treasury to alter the size of note issue for periods of two years at a time by laying a formal minute before Parliament, and in effect enabled the Treasury and the Bank to continue to increase the note issue at their discretion. Parliament could intervene, but is unlikely to do so even though the rapid increase in the size of the note issue has caused a great deal of concern among those people who have attributed our inflationary ills to this phenomenal increase. The note issue must, however, be seen in the context of the money supply as a whole and this is discussed in III. Unless the note issue is increased as bank deposits increase and as the gross national product expands, the banks could find themselves in the ludicrous position of not being able to meet their depositors' needs for cash. They would be able to allow their customers to draw cheques which transferred bank balances from one bank to another but would not have enough notes in their tills to pay out in cash.

8. Legal tender. The term legal tender applies to any form of money which must by law be accepted in payment of a debt. In Britain, Bank of England notes are legal tender for any amount, and so too is the £1 coin. The 50 pence piece must be accepted up to £10. As far as the smaller coins are concerned, a creditor must accept cupro-nickel coins for up to £5 and bronze coins up to 20 pence.

No one can be forced to accept payment by cheque or by postal order as they are not legal tender, but a creditor may elect to do so.

9. The gold reserves. In 1939, the Bank of England's stock of gold, amounting to approximately £300 million, was transferred from the issue department of the Bank to the Exchange Equalisation Account which was also the responsibility of the Bank. No longer was this gold to be held as backing for the note issue. Instead, it was to be used as backing for sterling in the foreign exchange market together with the Bank's reserves of foreign currency. Since 1932 when the Exchange Equalisation Account was set up, the Bank of England had used the foreign currency reserves to buy sterling when it was weak to keep up its exchange value and added to these reserves by buying foreign currencies with sterling when sterling was strong. Since 1939 both gold and foreign currency (the gold and currency reserves) have been used in this way. These official reserves now stand (February 1984) at $18,000 million, i.e. about £13,500 million.

PROGRESS TEST 2

1. Why were coins made of gold and silver and other valuable metals freely accepted as a medium of exchange? **(1)**

2. What is meant by debasing the coinage? **(3)**

3. Have modern-day coins any intrinsic value? **(1)**

4. How did bank notes originate? **(5)**

5. When and how were the note issues of the private banks taken over by the Bank of England? **(6)**

6. What is the fiduciary issue and how is it controlled? **(7)**

7. Does it matter that the fiduciary issue has risen from £260 million in 1928 to £11,500 million in 1984? **(7)**

8. What is meant by the term "legal tender" and what constitutes legal tender in Britain today? **(8)**

9. What are the gold and currency reserves and how are they used? **(9)**

CHAPTER III

Money in a Modern Society

DEPOSIT BANKING

1. Creation of deposits. The goldsmiths created new deposits by lending some of the gold and silver coin deposited with them. The customers who borrowed the money did so in order to carry out transactions and thus they passed it on to others who, quite possibly, deposited their money with the same goldsmith. As only a modest proportion of the gold and silver deposited was likely to be demanded back by the depositors at any one time, this process of creating deposits could go on and on, especially if new supplies of gold and silver were forthcoming. It was greatly aided, of course, by the introduction and general acceptance of bank-notes which could be used in making loans as an alternative to gold and silver coins. This was the origin of the pyramid of credit which has been built up over the centuries and which today is represented by the sterling deposits of about £160,000 million held by banks in the United Kingdom. These deposits are credit in the sense that they are sums of money lent by the current and deposit account holders to the banks and in that they have been created over the years through the process of bank lending and through the creation of notes and coins by the Bank of England.

2. Restrictions on the private banks. In an attempt to ensure that the Bank of England predominated as the major bank in Britain, various Acts of Parliament were passed (*see* VI and VII) which restricted the number of partners that a private bank could have and which in the early nineteenth century restricted the power of banks to issue their own notes if they established themselves in the London area. If the London banks were unable to issue notes, it was thought that they would not be able to make loans and hence their growth as banks would be greatly restricted. However, this did not allow for the fact that cheques and bills of exchange were being increasingly used and thus deposit banking was facilitated.

The term deposit banking was used to describe the system whereby banks accepted deposits as before, but made loans by permitting their customers to draw cheques or bills in excess of their balances. They either overdrew their current accounts up to prescribed limits or loan accounts were opened and their current accounts credited with a set sum of money. The ability of the banks to create credit was therefore no longer limited by the availability of gold and silver coins nor by their note issues, though naturally they still had to ensure that they kept adequate reserves of coin or of other banks' notes (usually Bank of England notes) so that they could meet their depositors' demands for cash.

Without the system of deposit banking and the creation of the pyramid of credit, industry and commerce, and hence our national income, could not have developed in the way they have to give us the standard of living we now enjoy.

THE PRESENT-DAY MONEY SUPPLY

3. Cash and bank deposits. In most developed economies cash and cheques are the generally acceptable means of payment for transactions. By cash, we mean notes and coin, which in the United Kingdom are Bank of England notes and coin. Such notes and coin are usually defined by law as legal tender, i.e. they must be acceptable within certain limits in payment for goods. Clearly this cash fulfils all the functions of money and is therefore part of the money supply.

Cheques on the other hand, cannot really be classified as part of the money supply, but they are a means of transferring the ownership of money. The form of money which they transfer is in fact bank deposits, and it is these that account for the major part of our money supply. As to precisely which bank deposits should be included as part of the money supply, there has been much controversy. For instance, should time deposits, e.g. deposit accounts as distinct from current account balances, be included in the money supply? It could be argued that anyone who has a time deposit may feel at liberty to draw a cheque overdrawing his current account knowing that a switch can be made from his deposit account if necessary. What about the wholesale deposits which the banks borrow in the money market and which represent investments by their owners rather than funds which they may want to use for transactions? What about the person who has an overdraft facility and draws a cheque in the knowledge that he can overdraw his account? Should the total of overdraft limits be included in the money supply?

4. Near-money assets. Many assets very closely resemble money, and may well be regarded as money by their holders. For instance, a postal order or money order is as good as cash to the holder, for he knows that he has only to take it to the post office in order to encash it. But it is not "true" money until he has encashed it and that is the essential difference between money and near-money assets. A near-money asset has to be converted into money, i.e. notes and coin or a bank deposit, before it can be used as money. Other examples of near-money assets are national savings certificates, Treasury bills, building society deposits or shares, shares in public companies, and insurance policies. The existence of near-money does mean that the quantity of true money in existence can be less. If a person holds some near-money assets then he will not feel the necessity to hold as much cash or have as large a deposit in the bank for emergency needs. A loss may be incurred in turning a near-money asset into money, whereas money will exchange for its full value. For instance when they are sold, the market value of stocks and shares may be well below the price that was paid for them. There may also be some delay in converting near-money to money and this is especially so if there is an agreed period of notice required before a withdrawal can be made.

5. Measures of money. In order to successfully carry out its monetary policy, it is necessary for the Government to measure the money stock in a number of ways. It needs to have measures reflecting the stock of assets available for transactions purposes as well as others reflecting the broad liquidity position of the private sector of the community. There are in fact five measures of narrow money held predominantly for spending immediately or in the near future on goods and services, i.e. for transactions, and four measures of broad money held both for transactions and as a store of value. The five narrow measures relate more to money as a medium of exchange, while the broader measures relate to many functioning as a store of value as well. As we shall see, some of the broader measures include some assets which might well be regarded as near-money rather than money itself:

(a) The narrow monetary aggregates are:

    (i) *Notes and coin.* This is the narrowest measure of all and is simply the total of notes and coin in circulation with the public.

    (ii) M_0. This consists of the total of notes and coin in circulation with the public, plus the banks' till money, plus their *operational* balances with the Bank of England. This is sometimes referred to as the wide monetary base, i.e. the cash base of the banks, and is not to be confused with the broader measures of money.

(*iii*) NIBM$_1$. Notes and coin plus UK private-sector non-interest-bearing sterling sight deposits in UK banks.

(*vi*) M$_1$. Notes and coin plus UK private-sector sterling sight deposits in UK banks.

(*v*) M$_2$. Notes and coin plus UK private-sector non-interest-bearing sterling sight deposits in UK banks plus interest-bearing deposits held by the private sector in UK banks and building societies for transactions purposes.

(*b*) The broad monetary aggregates are:

(*i*) Sterling M$_3$. This comprises M$_1$ plus private-sector sterling time bank deposits plus private-sector holdings of sterling bank certificates of deposit.

(*ii*) M$_3$. This comprises sterling M$_3$ plus private-sector foreign-currency bank deposits.

(*iii*) PSL$_1$. This includes M$_1$ plus private-sector sterling time bank deposits with an original maturity of up to two years plus private-sector holdings of sterling bank certificates of deposit plus private-sector holdings of money-market instruments (bank bills, Treasury bills, local authority deposits) and certficates of tax deposit.

(*vi*) PSL$_2$. This is equal to PSL$_1$ plus private-sector holdings of building society deposits (excluding term shares and SAYE) and national savings instruments (excluding certificates, SAYE and other longer-term deposits), and less building society holdings of money-market instruments and bank deposits etc.

TABLE I. UNITED KINGDOM MONEY SUPPLY, FEBRUARY 1984
(£ million)

Notes and coin	11,531
M$_0$	12,888
M$_1$	42,492
NIBM$_1$	30,548
M$_2$	118,429
Sterling M$_3$	118,215
M$_3$	101,140
PSL$_1$	102,660
PSL$_2$	168,827

Source: Bank of England Quarterly Bulletin

The totals of these monetary and liquidity aggregates as at February 1984 are shown in Table I.

PROGRESS TEST 3

1. How did the goldsmiths create new deposits? **(1)**
2. What is meant by the pyramid of credit? **(1)**
3. Why were the private banks precluded from issuing notes in the London area in the early nineteenth century?   **(2)**
4. What is meant by deposit banking and in what way has it led to the expansion of British industry and trade?   **(2)**
5. Are cheques money?   **(3)**
6. What are near-money assets and in what ways do they differ from money?   **(4)**
7. Distinguish between narrow and broad measures of money. **(5)**
8. Define M_0, M_1, M_2, and sterling M_3.   **(5)**

PART TWO

SAVINGS AND LENDING INSTITUTIONS

CHAPTER IV

Savings and Investment

SAVINGS IN THE UNITED KINGDOM

1. Savings defined. By the term saving, we mean refraining from spending. Any money which we have saved and set aside for use in the future we refer to as our savings. Money is saved if it is not spent, and it does not necessarily have to be placed in a bank, a building society or any other financial institution or used to purchase stocks and shares in order to justify the use of the term.

2. Sources of savings. In 1981 personal saving amounted to £22,604 million but after allowing for depreciation, stock appreciation and addition to tax reserves this amount was reduced to £16,013 million. This was 7 per cent of total personal income in that year. This may seem a surprisingly high proportion, but it is not always realised that an individual saves not only by depositing money and buying securities but also by paying premiums on an assurance policy or by contributing to a superannuation scheme. Money used to keep up an assurance policy is not being used to buy goods or services. It is taken by the assurance company and used by them to buy stocks and shares or in some way lent in order to produce as high an income as possible to the company. When the policy matures or some event occurs to cause the assurance company to pay up, the beneficiary receives a lump sum which can then be spent. In the meantime it has been saved. As the assurance companies handle millions of pounds of people's savings every day they are thus an important channel through which money flows from the individual to industry. Likewise, pension contributions constitute a large sum of money which pension funds are able to use profitably by purchasing securities or making loans. The employee gets his savings back (plus possibly some money which the employer has saved for him as his contribution to the pension fund) as a pension when he retires.

Personal saving is extremely important in that the individual spends most of his money on consumer goods and, during periods of inflation when the demand for these goods is excessive, anything that can be done to encourage him to save rather than spend is going to help combat that inflation. The term personal saving refers not only to individuals but also all unincorporated business concerns (self-employed people, one-man businesses and partnerships), non-profit-making bodies such as trade unions and charitable trusts, and life assurance companies and superannuation funds.

A large contribution to the nation's saving also comes from industry and commerce. This represents the undistributed profits and reserves of companies and in 1981 amounted to £24,813 million. However, after provisions for depreciation, stock appreciation and additions to tax reserves this was reduced to £1,533 million.

Local and central government and the nationalised industries all spend more than they receive in income these days and they have to borrow to bridge the gap. This borrowing comes from the savings of both the personal sector and industry and commerce.

3. National savings. This term is used to mean that part of personal savings (and possibly to some extent corporate savings) which is deposited with the National Savings Bank or is used to buy national savings certificates, premium savings bonds, or British savings bonds or is saved through the Save As You Earn scheme. The national savings movement has deliberately sought, to encourage the individual to save, by advertising and by offering favourable terms. The total of national savings at March 1982 is shown in Table II, together with a breakdown into the type of national savings.

THE NEED FOR INVESTMENT

4. Investment. The word "investment" has been deliberately avoided so far in this chapter because of the confusion which can so easily be caused by the fact that the word has two meanings. On the one hand, the word can be used to mean a deposit with a financial institution or the purchase of a security, e.g. an investment in a Trustee Savings Bank or an investment in national savings certificates or "on the Stock Exchange". On the other hand, to an economist, the word "investment" means the acquisition of a new capital asset such as a factory or machinery. It is the latter type of investment, capital investment, which is so important to the community. This investment provides the means whereby additional goods and services can be produced, i.e. the gross national product (the national income) can be expanded. Our standard of living today has depended a great deal upon the capital investment in factories, plant and equipment, roads, railways, bridges etc. that was carried out in the past.

TABLE II. NATIONAL SAVINGS IN THE UK MARCH 1982
(£ million)

National Savings Certificates	12,333
British Savings Bonds	286
Premium Bonds	1,506
Other stocks on the National Savings Stock Register	842
Save As You Earn	657
National Savings Stamps	1
National Savings Bank:	
Ordinary account	1,702
Investment account	2,992
Total National Savings	20,319

Source: Annual Abstract of Statistics

5. Savings must equal investment. In order that capital investment can be carried out, an equal amount of money must be saved. This is because those persons who are involved in the construction of a capital asset, a bricklayer building a factory for instance, or in making goods, e.g. bricks, that are used in its construction, receive an income. Naturally they will wish to spend most if not all of this income in buying consumer goods; but they have not produced any consumer goods themselves. Unless, therefore, the community as a whole refrains from spending a total sum equal to the value of the capital investment carried out, the demand for consumer goods will exceed the supply. Table III shows the total of capital investment in the UK in 1981 by types of investment and by the sectors of industry which carried out the investment.

Hence saving and investment are vital to the community and so are the savings and lending institutions which facilitate both the saving and the investment.

Obviously both the saving and the investment need not be carried out by the same person or corporate body. A firm might well put

TABLE III. CAPITAL INVESTMENT IN THE UK 1981
(£ million)

BY TYPE OF INVESTMENT

Buses and coaches	279
Other road vehicles	3,759
Railway rolling stock	151
Ships	253
Aircraft	145
Plant and machinery	15,581
Dwellings	5,186
Other new buildings and works	12,313
Transfer costs of land and buildings	1,710
	39,377

BY INDUSTRY GROUP

Agriculture, forestry and fishing	843
Petroleum and natural gas	2,847
Mining and quarrying (excluding petroleum and natural gas)	837
Manufacturing	6,227
Construction	582
Gas, electricity and water	2,376
Transport and communication	4,090
Distributive trades	2,601
Other service industries	7,524
Dwellings	5,186
Social services	1,805
Other public services	2,749
Transfer costs of land and buildings	1,710
	£39,377

Source: Annual Abstracts of Statistics.

money into reserve and use it in due course to acquire some new capital asset, in which case it does both the saving and the investing, but this is not always the case. The individual who pays premiums on an assurance policy is enabling the assurance company to lend money to industry, either by buying shares or by way of loan or debenture, to enable industry to acquire capital assets.

The financial institutions provide much of the capital which industry requires to carry out capital investment, i.e. they accept deposits, which are savings, and either directly or indirectly pass on the savings to industry or the public sector for investment purposes.

PROGRESS TEST 4

1. What is meant by saving? **(1)**
2. In what ways does an individual save? **(2)**
3. Do companies save? **(2)**
4. What are national savings? **(3)**
5. Distinguish between the two meanings of the word investment. **(4)**
6. Why must we save in order to invest? **(5)**
7. Are saving and investment necessarily carried out by the same person? **(5)**

CHAPTER V

Savings Media

CHANNELS FOR SAVINGS

1. Introduction. As we saw in IV, the National Savings movement plays an important part in the collection of savings from the personal sector for use by the public sector in bridging its gap between income and expenditure. There are many other channels, however, through which savings flow from the saver to the company or to the public sector, where the investment is carried out. We now need to look at the savings media in greater detail.

2. The National Savings Bank. The Post Office Savings Bank was founded in 1861 under the control of the Post Office and with its functions and organisation laid down by statute. In 1969, when the Post Office became a public corporation and was no longer a Government department, the Post Office Savings Bank was hived off from the Post Office and continued to be run by the Civil Service within the new Department of National Savings. The bank was renamed the National Savings Bank. It continued to use 22,000 post offices and sub-offices for its transactions with its depositors. With such a large network of offices located in even the smallest towns and villages it offers the convenience of location to its customers plus the advantage of being able to carry out transactions on Saturdays. However, post offices offer a wide range of services other than those of the National Savings Bank which can cause congestion and delay for the Savings Bank customers.

The National Savings Bank provides two types of account facilities: ordinary accounts and investment accounts. Ordinary accounts may be opened for or by anyone over seven years of age with a maximum deposit of £10,000. For over 100 years interest at the rate of 2½ per cent was paid on these accounts, but since 1971 the Government has been able to vary the rate by statutory instrument and at the time of writing it stands at 3 per cent for balances up to £500 and 6 per cent for balances at or above that figure. Interest is exempt from income tax up to £70 in any one year. Up to £100 may be withdrawn on demand at any post office or sub-office operating

National Savings Bank facilities.

A depositor may open an investment account in which the maximum deposit is £200,000 (in addition to a possible £10,000 on ordinary account). One month's notice of withdrawal is required and the rate of interest payable has varied since this type of account was introduced in 1966. The rate is dependent upon the income earned by the Investment Account Fund in which the deposits are invested, and in June 1984 stood at $9\frac{1}{4}$ per cent whereas the banks were paying only $5\frac{1}{4}$ per cent on deposit accounts.

Depositors may make withdrawals from both ordinary and investment accounts by crossed warrants which can be used in the same way as a cheque. They can also arrange for standing order payments and may make transfers to a National Girobank Account or for the purchase of national savings certificates, British savings bonds, premium bonds or any of the Government stock listed on the National Savings Stock Register.

Employers may remit to the National Savings Bank sums of money deducted regularly from employees' wages or salaries for the credit of ordinary accounts opened specially for each individual.

The deposits of the National Savings Bank have to be kept by the National Debt Office in two separate funds and invested by that office in prescribed public sector securities. The depositors' capital, and interest thereon, is therefore guaranteed by the State. Some of the bank's operating expenses come from the earnings from these investments but a proportion of the expenses of the National Savings Department comes out of public funds.

3. The National Girobank. In 1968, the Post Office introduced the National Giro (renamed National Girobank in 1978) in order to provide a means whereby depositors with the system could arrange transfers to the accounts of other depositors and might draw cheques in favour of payees who are not Girobank account holders. Account holders may also make transfers by standing orders to other Girobank accounts and to clearing bank and trustee savings bank accounts. They can also arrange to have their salaries credited to their giro accounts. The Giro originated as a money transmission service, but with the change in its name its services were expanded to include personal loans, cheque books and cheque guarantee cards, budget accounts and travellers' cheques. These developments greatly increased the bank's popularity and its customers' balances have risen substantially; and to the extent that these balances are left outstanding they provide an important source of savings for use by the public sector.

Unlike the National Savings Bank which is now operated by the

Department for National Savings, the Girobank is owned and run by the Post Office Corporation. Together with the system of postal orders and money orders, the giro provides a means of transmitting money through the Post Office.

4. Trustee Savings Banks. Although there were a number of savings banks in existence before 1817, the Savings Bank Act of that year really marks the beginning of the development of Trustee Savings Banks as they are known today. The Act provided that depositors' funds were to be invested in a separate account at the Bank of England and managed by the National Debt Commissioners who would pay a fixed rate of interest on the deposits. The treasurers, trustees or managers were to provide their services on a voluntary basis. Another Act, the Trustee Savings Bank Act 1863, established the legal liability of trustees and managers, limiting it to matters arising from their own acts or their wilful neglect or default. In 1819 there were 465 separate savings banks in the British Isles but by 1974 they had been consolidated to seventy-two. Further consolidation then took place as a result of the implementation of the Page Report recommendations of 1973 when they were reduced to eighteen banks under a Central Trustee Savings Bank.

In 1983 the number of Trustee Savings Banks was reduced still further to just four banks under a holding company and their services have become so diversified that they can no longer be considered as savings banks and are therefore considered in detail in VII in the context of commercial banking. In the context of this present chapter the fact that at any one time a very substantial sum of deposits is in the hands of the Trustee Savings Banks makes it important to include them as a source of savings for use by both the private and public sectors.

ASSURANCE COMPANIES AND PENSION FUNDS

5. Assurance policies. The life funds of the assurance companies have increased very rapidly over recent years and account for much of the personal savings that have accrued in the period.

NOTE: The term "assurance" is applied to life and endowment cover whereas the term "insurance" is applied to other types of cover for risks such as fire, theft and damage which may or may not occur.

Endowment polices account for most of the premiums paid for life assurance. These are policies which provide for a set sum of money (with or without profits) to be paid to the policyholder if he survives to a certain date or to his next of kin if he dies before then. Whole life policies provide a benefit only upon the death of the assured. Life assurance (both whole life and endowment policies) for which premiums are collected from door to door is known as industrial life assurance, whereas other life policies are known as ordinary life assurance.

6. Friendly societies. Some friendly societies function very much like industrial assurance companies and operate under the Industrial Assurance Acts, while others operate entirely within the Friendly Societies Acts. The latter type exists to provide help to their members and their families when in need, possibly through sickness or unemployment or retirement, or upon the death of a member. They take voluntary subscriptions from members.

7. Pension funds. Where an employee contributes to a pension fund he is in effect saving, because he is deferring some of his expenditure until he retires. To the extent that the firm also contributes to the pension fund it is similarly saving, but this saving is not on its own account but on behalf of the employee. Pension funds are mostly invested in stocks and shares and constitute a major part of the flow of savings that is used by industry to carry out capital investment. Some of the larger companies run their own pension schemes while others have schemes run for them by assurance companies. In 1981 the net income, after administrative costs and payment of pension benefits, of funded pension schemes (including those of life assurance companies) was £12,824 million.

LOCAL AUTHORITIES

8. Types of loans. Investments in local authorities have increased considerably in importance in recent years. New types of borrowing instruments have been introduced which have attracted loans from institutional lenders both at home and abroad, with the consequence that the importance to local authorities of the small private lender has declined, though this type of investor still accounts for an appreciable part of local authority debt.

For years the traditional type of small local authority loan has been the mortgage loan which attracted a fixed rate of interest payable half-yearly. These have tended to be replaced by local authority bonds which are simpler and more flexible but, like the mortgage loan, are non-negotiable. Other non-negotiable loans by local authorities are taken on a temporary basis (for less than one year) for large sums against a simple receipt. Negotiable securities issued by local authorities include negotiable bonds similar to local authority bonds but negotiable in the London money market; stock similar to Treasury stock and bought and sold on the Stock Exchange; and local authority bills which are rather similar to Treasury bills.

BUILDING SOCIETIES

9. Functions. A building society, like other financial institutions, borrows money and lends it out at higher rates of interest than it pays for it. It accepts deposits on share accounts.

The shareholders are the owners of the societies but they are paid interest, not dividends. The societies are in effect mutual societies in as much as they are non-profit-making institutions. Many of the depositors are also borrowers on mortgage. However, it is not essential for a mortgage holder to be a shareholder, though shareholders do get preferential treatment in the allocation of mortgages during a period when funds are scarce.

10. Tax advantages. The building societies pay a composite rate of income tax based on an agreed favourable rate and this enables them to pay interest to their shareholders free of income tax at the basic rate. When "grossed-up" to allow for the income tax which a person receiving interest on any other type of investment would have to pay, the building society rates are very attractive, especially to the small saver. So too are the easy withdrawal terms and the possibility of preferential treatment when applying for a mortgage. This advantage of paying interest net of tax is to be extended to the banks from April 1985.

Interest paid by borrowers on their mortgages is also given preferential treatment by the Inland Revenue in that it can be set off against income for income tax purposes, and in most cases mortgage repayments are now actually paid net of tax at the standard rate.

The rates of interest both paid and received by building societies bear some relationship to other market rates of interest. When the banks raise or lower their base rates the building societies do not immediately adjust their rates but they will tend to do so in the long run. What is of greater significance is that the building societies must compete with other types of investment, especially national savings, if they are to attract a continuous flow of new funds and thus be able to provide mortgages. When yields on the various forms of national savings change, so too will building society rates of interest.

7. Trustee status. Those building societies whose total assets and structure of assets comply with certain criteria laid down in the Building Societies Act 1962 may claim trustee status. This means that trustees of money belonging to other people may by law invest the money in these particular building societies if they choose to do so. To obtain this status, a society must have total assets of at least £500,000, a liquidity (cash and investments) ratio of at least $7\frac{1}{2}$ per cent of total assets and general reserves of at least $2\frac{1}{2}$ per cent of total assets ($2\frac{1}{2}$ per cent if assets exceed £100 million).

UNIT AND INVESTMENT TRUSTS

12. Unit trusts. Investment in a unit trust enables a saver to spread his risks over a wide range of industries. An individual who has set aside, say, £100 for investment would find it unprofitable to buy a small number of shares in a number of different companies through a stockbroker. However, an investment of that sum in a unit trust would give him a share in the total investment in stocks and shares by the trust. A decline in the fortunes of one industry would be offset by an improvement in the income from and capital appreciation of other shares held by the unit trust. The total assets of a unit trust are divided into units and the earnings of each individual unit are calculated by dividing the total earnings of the trust by the number of units. The managers of the trust are responsible for the day-to-day administration of the trust and, in addition, trustees are appointed (usually a bank), who hold the trust's assets on behalf of its members.

The day-to-day market value of units is determined by supply and demand on the Stock Exchange for the stocks and shares in which the unit trust's funds are invested. Blocks of new units are offered for purchase by advertisements in the daily press from time to time, the money received for them being invested in additional stocks and shares, and it is also possible for a saver to purchase units by regular monthly subscription for a set period of years. Many subscription schemes provide for assurance cover which guarantees that in the event of the death of the subscriber his next of kin will receive a sum of money related to the amount that was expected to be subscribed over the period of the scheme. Alternatively, such a scheme may guarantee that the units will be worth at least a set minimum sum at the end of the period.

An investor in a unit trust would be wise to regard his investment as long term, in that the market value of his units will vary up and down in line with the value of stocks and shares. Whereas an investment in a building society can be withdrawn intact at short notice, it is not always so in the case of money invested in unit trusts. If the Stock Exchange values are down when the investor wishes to liquidate his investment, he has to consider seriously whether it would be wise to hold on until share prices improve. However despite this uncertainty, unit trusts are very popular and the unit trust movement has grown rapidly in recent years.

13. Investment trusts. An investment trust is a limited company which uses its shareholders' funds, and money borrowed on loan, to invest in stocks and shares. Unlike a unit trust, it is not a trust in the legal sense of the term. The shareholders receive dividends which are paid out of the dividends received by the trust from its investments. Shareholders tend to have larger holdings than those of investors in unit trusts and the investment trusts are not in the market for small savings in the way unit trusts are. The shareholders buy and sell their shares through a stockbroker in the same way as shareholders in other companies.

HIRE-PURCHASE COMPANIES

14. Finance houses. The majority of hire-purchase finance is provided by the larger hire-purchase companies that are members of the Finance Houses Association.

These, and the smaller houses that also provide this type of finance, borrow money from the banks and accept deposits from industrial and commercial companies and insurance companies and also from private individuals. The amount borrowed from small savers is not very significant in relation to their total liabilities. The larger houses set a fairly high minimum to the size of deposit they are prepared to accept and most deposits are at three or six months' notice. Some of the larger houses are owned by London clearing banks and rely for their funds upon their parent banks.

Most of the money lent is provided on hire-purchase terms, i.e. the investment is payable on the whole of the sum borrowed for the whole of the period of the loan. This means that the true rate of interest is virtually twice as high as the nominal rate quoted to the borrower. For instance, if £1,000 is borrowed over a two-year period at 12 per cent the interest amounts to £240; but this interest is on an average loan of approximately £500 because during the first year the loan ranges from £1,000 to £500 and in the second year from £500 to nil. In fact, the "true" rate works out at about $23\frac{1}{2}$ per cent per annum but does include the administrative cost of collecting the instalments on possibly a weekly basis and the commission, if any, payable to the retailer. The goods can be repossessed within certain limits so that the loan is at least partially secured.

For professional people, the finance houses have tended to offer the alternative of an instalment loan which attracts no right of repossession should the borrower default. The loan of an agreed sum of money is made based on the borrower's credit-worthiness which is assessed on his past record as a borrower (status enquiries are made) and the fact that he has a regular income. Repayments are usually made by banker's standing order. The loans may also be revolving, i.e. when a certain proportion of a debt has been repaid the borrower may automatically borrow an additional sum that will take the debt back to its original amount.

The finance houses also lend to industry to assist in the purchase of items of machinery and equipment and, for instance, to enable a firm to build a new showroom for the display of goods which may be sold on hire-purchase terms (in which the particular hire-purchase company's facilities would be made available to buyers). Such lending may well go considerably beyond the two- or three-year period that is normal for hire-purchase finance.

COMMERCIAL BANKS

The evolution, functions and services of the commercial banks are described in great detail in subsequent chapters. The purpose of referring to them in this chapter is to draw attention to the importance of them as institutions which accept deposits, and hence to some extent savings, and to show the essential differences between them and other savings institutions.

15. Types of deposits. In a similar way to the National Savings Banks and the Trustee Savings Banks, the commercial banks accept deposits from their customers, but unlike these other banks, most of the total sum deposited with them is from industrial and commercial depositors. This does not mean that the commercial banks have few private customers (far from it: they cater for millions of them) but the sums of money involved are much greater for firms than for individuals.

In their so-called retail branches, as distinct from the wholesale activities of their Head Offices, the commercial banks offer two main types of account to depositors, current accounts and deposit accounts. Current account holders receive no interest on their accounts (apart from the new high interest accounts), but they can draw cheques on them and use the credit giro service, and they can withdraw some or all of their balances on demand. Deposit account holders, on the other hand, do receive interest on their accounts but do not normally draw cheques on the accounts nor use the credit giro system for paying in credits and, technically, they are required to give seven days' notice or more of their intention to make withdrawals from their accounts. In reality, the banks do not insist on this period of notice but will deduct seven days' interest in lieu of notice.

The commercial banks also operate savings accounts for their customers with or without a home safe that can be used for savings. The number of these accounts is comparatively small.

It is also possible for customers to deposit large sums of money, amounting to at least £10,000, on a fixed-term basis at more favourable rates of interest than that paid on normal deposit accounts.

16. Interest rates. Despite the fact that their interest rates are generally less favourable than those of some other institutions, especially the building societies, the commercial banks have attracted personal savings and must not be overlooked in the context of savings institutions. A high proportion of the money on deposit accounts is from private depositors and in their evidence to the Committee to review National Savings (in 1973), the Committee of London Clearing Bankers estimated that 40–45 per cent of deposit account holders do not have a current account.

To the extent that current account holders also keep balances for day-to-day needs (and many of them in excess of their needs) they, with deposit account holders, provide a very large pool indeed of deposits which can be used by the banks to provide commerce and industry with the capital it needs.

17. Provision of credit. Approximately 70 per cent of a commercial bank's deposits are lent to private, industrial and commercial borrowers, while most of the rest is lent either directly or indirectly to the Government.

18 Other bank services. The commercial banks provide speedy, efficient payments mechanisms for their current account customers, and the main banks jointly run the London Clearing House through which the majority of debit and credit items are channelled. The debit items comprise hundreds of millions of cheques drawn by the customers every year, while the credit items are the giro credits paid in at branches throughout Britain and standing orders and other credits paid by a bank on behalf of its customers to customers of other banks.

PROGRESS TEST 5

1. Describe the services which the National Savings Bank provides for its customers.   **(2)**

2. The National Girobank is not a savings bank; how then can it be said to be an important source of savings for use in the public sector?   **(3)**

3. What is the difference between a whole life policy and an endowment policy?   **(5)**

4. Define a friendly society.   **(6)**

5. How does a pension fund contribute to the development of industry?   **(7)**

6. What are the main types of local authority securities?   **(8)**

7. Who owns a building society?   **(9)**

8. What factors determine the rates of interest paid by building societies?   **(10)**

9. What is a unit trust?   **(12)**

10. What is an investment trust?   **(13)**

11. Describe the sources of funds employed by the hire-purchase finance houses.   **(14)**

12. In what ways can it be said that the hire-purchase companies help industry and commerce?   **(14)**

13. Do the commercial banks attract personal savings?   **(15, 16)**

14. To what extent do the commercial banks lend money to industry and commerce and to the Government?   **(17)**

PART THREE

THE BRITISH BANKING SYSTEM

CHAPTER VI

The Central Bank

THE EVOLUTION OF THE BANK OF ENGLAND

1. The hub of the banking system. In every country where there is a developed banking system the main bank, the hub of the system, is the central bank. In the UK the central bank is the Bank of England, which was established in 1694. The central bank's functions are in the main quite different from those of the commercial and other banks and, in that it is the Government's bank and the bankers' bank, it has a controlling influence over the banks as a whole.

2. The establishment of the Bank of England. The Bank of England was established under charter with the very privileged position of being the first joint-stock banking company. This meant that it could have a large number of shareholders and was not restricted to being a partnership, as were the other banks. This was a *quid pro quo* for a loan to the king of £1,200,000 and it was this loan which established the Bank as the Government's bank.

From the beginning, the Bank of England accepted money on deposit, issued its own notes and made loans in the same way that the other banks did, and was able to increase its business more rapidly than them as a result of the Bank of England Act 1709 which provided that no bank other than the Bank of England could have more than six partners. At the beginning of the nineteenth century there were more than 400 small private banks which depended greatly on the support of the Bank of England if they ran into financial difficulties, as many of them did, especially during the crisis of 1825.

Because many banks had to close their doors, confidence in the banking system and in the system of credit creation was greatly affected, and legislation was introduced, especially that of 1826, 1833 and 1844, to encourage the establishment of larger banking units on the one hand and to control the note issue on the other. The 1826 and 1833 Acts will be considered in the next chapter, in that they influenced the development of commercial banks; the 1844 Bank Charter Act is however important as a milestone in the development of the central bank.

3. The Bank Charter Act 1844. This Act had three main provisions.

(*a*) To divide the Bank of England into two separate departments, the Banking Department and the Issue Department and to publish a weekly return.

(*b*) To permit the Bank to make a fiduciary issue of £14 million of notes to be backed by Government securities. Every note issued above this limit was to be backed by gold.

(*c*) Ultimately to centralise the note issue in the hands of the Bank of England by gradually extinguishing private note issues as the private banks became bankrupt or amalgamated with other banks. The last surviving private note-issuing bank was Fox, Fowler and Company, which amalgamated with Lloyds Bank in 1921.

Thus the Bank of England gradually assumed responsibility for the currency supply and as the holder of the country's gold reserves in that, apart from the relatively small fiduciary issue, it had to hold gold as backing for the note issue. The banking system as a whole depended upon the gold backing, and by helping the private banks during money market crises in the latter part of the nineteenth century, the Bank of England was able to inspire world-wide confidence in itself as lender of last resort. It had gradually taken on those functions which today are recognised as being those of a central bank. It started off in 1694 as a commercial bank and then in the second half of the nineteenth century gradually stopped competing with the other banks and concentrated on its new role as the first central bank in the world.

THE BANK OF ENGLAND'S POWERS AND INFLUENCE

4. Nationalisation of the Bank of England. The Bank was nationalised in 1946, when the conduct of the Bank was placed in the hands of a Court of Directors headed by the Governor of the Bank of England. The directors are appointed by the Crown and the Governor and senior officers work in close liaison with the Treasury.

The Act of 1946 gave the Bank of England very wide powers of control over the other banks so that it no longer had to rely on their voluntary co-operation as it had done previously, particularly during the Second World War. The extent of these powers can be seen from the following extract from the Act.

"The Bank, if they think it necessary in the public interest, may request information from and make recommendations to bankers, and may, if so authorised by the Treasury, issue directions to any banker for the purpose of securing that effect is given to any such request or recommendation:
Provided that:

(a) no such request or recommendations shall be made with respect to the affairs of any particular customer of a banker, and
(b) before authorising the issue of any such directions the Treasury shall give the banker concerned, or such person as appears to them to represent him, an opportunity of making representations with respect thereto."

5. Banking Act 1979. The Bank of England was given even stronger powers of control over the banking system by the Banking Act 1979. This Act brought the recognition and licensing of banks and deposit-taking institutions generally under the direct control of the Bank which was also given the power to withdraw recognition or licence. Such powers were called for under the First EEC Directive on the Co-ordination of Banking Law which requires that all credit institutions should obtain authorisation before commencing activities and laid down certain criteria concerning capital, types of business and business reputations of directors which have to be fulfilled before authorisation can be granted.

The Act required all institutions already accepting deposits to apply to the Bank of England for permission to continue to do so and from then on all new deposit-taking institutions have had to apply for permission before starting up business. The 1979 Act distinguishes between two types of institution, a *recognised bank* and a *licensed deposit-taker*. To obtain recognised bank status, which gives an institution the right to call itself a bank, very stringent requirements are laid down in the Act and also the Bank of England is given considerable discretionary powers which enable it to use its own judgment in deciding whether or not to recognise a particular institution as a bank.

A licensed deposit-taker is an institution which meets the criteria laid down for permission to accept deposits, but does not match up to the requirements which would permit recognised bank status. All licensed deposit-takers must furnish the Bank with information which goes well beyond that provided in their balance sheets and must accept the Bank's statutory powers of supervision. As far as recognised banks are concerned these are less stringent but it must be remembered that the Bank of England has always the sanction of withdrawing a bank's licence if it is not satisfied with the way in which it is conducting its affairs. Since the 1979 Act the prudential supervision of the banking system has thus been very much tighter than ever before.

Another provision of the Banking Act 1979 was concerned with the establishment of a deposit protection Fund to which all banks and licensed deposit-takers have had to subscribe. In the event of failure by any such institution depositors are assured of receiving compensation from the fund of 75 per cent of their deposits up to a maximum deposit of £10,000, i.e. maximum compensation of £7,500:

6. Channels of communication. Quite apart from direct contact between the Bank of England and individual institutions within the Bank's supervising powers, there are regular channels of communication between the Bank of England and the other financial institutions in London, and through these it is able to discuss problems as they arise and seek compliance with its wishes. These channels include the two committees of the London Clearing Bankers (one of the chairmen of the banks and the other of general managers), the Accepting Houses' Association, the Discount Market Association and a number of other groups representing financial institutions.

In recent years, the Bank of England has publicised its activities far more than ever before through its quarterly bulletin and through its annual report. The bulletin is a valuable source of vital financial data.

FUNCTIONS OF THE BANK OF ENGLAND

7. The Government's bank. The Bank of England is responsible for running accounts for all the Government departments and it has been the Bank's general policy not to maintain accounts for individuals and firms in the private sector (the non-Government sector of the community). It has a few private sector accounts and has in recent years relaxed its policy to some extent by opening accounts for some commercial firms but, generally speaking, the Bank does not reckon to compete with the commercial banks.

8. The bankers' bank. By maintaining accounts with the Bank of England the other banks are able to settle transactions with one another and with the institutions in the public sector, and also to maintain current account balances which form part of their liquid reserves. The day-to-day settlement of transactions through the London Clearing House is facilitated by the banks being able to make payments from, and receive payments into, their accounts at the Bank of England. Some of the other functions listed below also provide services to the banks as customers of the Bank of England, e.g. the replacement of notes and coins. The reader should endeavour to look at each of these functions and determine to what extent they are services to the banks and services for, and on behalf of, the Government.

9. Lender of last resort. If the London money market is short of funds, the Bank of England must always come to its aid, though it will do so at its own price, i.e. it will determine the rate of interest at which it is prepared to buy bills or to lend. In Britain it is the London discount houses that have to seek the Bank's help as is explained later (*see* VIII, **4–6**). The Bank may choose to give either direct or indirect assistance in the market or may (rarely these days) force the discount houses to borrow from it for a minimum period of seven days. If the Bank decides to give direct assistance it will buy bills from the discount houses. Indirect assistance to the discount houses occurs when the Bank of England buys the bills from the banks and thus enables them to increase their lending (call money) to the discount houses.

10. Control of the currency issue. In conjunction with the Treasury, the Bank of England determines the size of the fiduciary issue and is responsible for the amount of the coinage. The note issue must be increased to meet seasonal demands, e.g. at Christmas and during the summer holiday period. All torn and dirty notes which are bundled up and sent to the Bank of England by the banks must be destroyed and replaced. There must be adequate coins of each denomination to satisfy the needs of the community. The banks' bullion departments obtain their requirements from the Bank of England and pay in any coins surplus to their needs.

11. Issue and redemption of Government stocks. The Bank is responsible for issuing all Government stocks, recording their ownership and paying the interest on them. It also makes the arrangements for maturing stocks to be redeemed.

These securities represent the main part of the national debt and their sale and redemption provides an important means whereby the Bank of England can manipulate the availability of funds and the level of interest rates in the long-term money market.

12. The Treasury bill tender. Each Friday, the Bank of England receives bids for the week's issue of Treasury bills and is responsible for allocating the bills to the highest bidders. It publicises the average rate of interest at which the bills have been allotted and this rate is a key indicator of the level of interest rates in the money market.

13. Maintaining the gold and currency reserves. The UK central reserve of gold and foreign currencies is kept by the Bank as backing for sterling in the foreign exchange market.

14. Operating the Exchange Equalisation Account. The gold and currency reserves referred to above are held in the exchange equalisation account which is run by the Bank. The account has been credited with a holding of Treasury bills, which the Bank can use as necessary to acquire sterling to sell on the foreign exchange market (i.e. the bills are sold for sterling in the money market). The sterling has to be paid (by crediting the accounts of the banks and other foreign exchange dealers) when foreign currency is purchased. When foreign currency is sold, then sterling is received in exchange and any surplus is used to pay off some of the Treasury bills.

By buying and selling foreign currencies in exchange for sterling, the Bank of England endeavours to keep the value of sterling in terms of other currencies stable. When the value of sterling falls, it buys sterling and sells other currencies, and when sterling is strong it buys foreign currencies with sterling. The student of economics will appreciate that by bringing about changes in the demand and supply situations it is possible to affect prices, i.e. the values of sterling in terms of other currencies.

15. Carrying out the Government's monetary policy. The Bank of England is the principal agent for the Government in pursuing its monetary policy. Not only is it reponsible for the fiduciary issue, but also through its controls over, and influences upon, the banks and other financial institutions, it is able to restrain or increase the total money supply.

The total of bank deposits, which account for the major part of the money supply (but depending upon which measure of the money stock is used), depends very considerably upon the ability of the banks to create credit. Before considering the devices the Bank of England uses in carrying out the monetary policy it is therefore necessary to examine how credit is created.

THE CREDIT CREATION PROCESS

16. Advances become deposits. When someone arranges a loan or
overdraft with a bank, he does so in order to buy something or to
settle a debt. He is not likely to borrow money and leave it idle on his
account for very long. The person who sells him the goods or receives
settlement for the debt will pay the money into his bank or pass it on
to someone else who will pay it into a bank. Assuming, therefore, that
the amount of money kept in the form of notes and coin remains
fairly static, we can say that every loan creates a deposit, not
necessarily with the bank that made the loan, but with the banking
system as a whole.

When the money that is lent comes back into the banking system in
this way, the bank receiving it will find that the item Cash in the
balance sheet has increased, because the cheque will, in passing
through the Bank Clearing House, increase the bank's balance at the
Bank of England. As the bank will keep only the minimum of cash (in
the tills and at the Bank of England) that it needs for its day-to-day
requirements (because cash is a non-profit-earning asset), it will want
to employ most of the new deposit in other ways so as to make a
profit. It must keep adequate liquid assets, but the remainder could
be used to make a loan. This loan would in turn create a deposit and a
sizeable proportion of the new deposit could be lent. This process can
go on until deposits have been increased by several times the amount
of the original advance; this is known as the credit creation multiplier.
The actual size of the multiplier cannot easily be determined, but for
the sake of simplicity and in order that the reader should grasp the
principle involved, let us assume that 20 per cent has to be held in the
form of reserve assets and work through the following example.

If a loan of £1,000,000 is made by Bank A to a customer and he
draws a cheque in favour of a customer of Bank B, the balance
sheet of Bank B will change as follows:

Bank B

Deposits + £1,000,000   Cash + £1,000,000

Assuming Bank B uses as much of this additional cash as possible
for additional advances the balance sheet will change as follows:

Bank B

Deposits + £1,000,000	Cash and
	other reserve assets + £200,000
	advances + £800,000

If the customer of Bank B who borrows £800,000 uses it to pay a debt to a customer of Bank C then Bank C's cash will increase by £800,000 and if it increases its advances as much as possible its balance sheet will change as follows:

Bank C

Deposits + £800,000	Cash and
	other reserve assets + £160,000
	advances + £640,000

We could then go on to assume that £640,000 found its way into Bank D and bank deposits as a whole will then have increased by £2,440,000 (£1,000,000 + £800,000 + £640,000). This process could go on and on until the amount of cash is too small to be re-lent and it would then be found that bank deposits had gone up by £5,000,000. Hence an original loan of £1,000,000 has created deposits five times as great, i.e. there is a multiplier of 5 *in our particular example.*

17. The size of the multiplier. A great deal of controversy has arisen in recent years concerning the size of the multiplier, and it would be inappropriate to consider this in detail in a study of Elements of Banking. The student will need to do so when he studies Monetary Economics in Stage II of the Banking Diploma examinations. It is sufficient at this stage to accept that bank lending does have a multiplier effect upon bank deposits and that if the Government wishes to control the money supply it is vital to control the ability of the banks to create credit.

The multiplier effect only operates when fresh cash comes into the banking system, e.g. when the public sector pays money to the private sector or funds come from abroad. If in our example above the £1,000,000 was paid to the customer of Bank A by a Government department, possibly in payment for armaments, then deposits could be created in the way suggested. If, however, the payment was from a customer of Bank Z then Bank A's credit-creating power would be at the expense of Bank Z who would have to reduce their advances in order to maintain the minimum reserve ratio. The net effect as far as the banking system as a whole is concerned would be to leave the level of deposits unchanged.

18. Government intervention. If through the flow of fresh cash into the banking system the banks are able to create credit, the Government can, through the Bank of England, intervene in the money market to pursue its particular monetary policy. If the Government's policy is to restrict the money supply, i.e. to mop up some of the fresh cash and stop the multiplier effect, the Bank of England will use open market operations to achieve this. If, on the other hand, the Government's monetary policy is one of expansion, the Bank of England will do nothing to stop the credit creation process and may even try to accelerate it by putting more cash into the banking system.

The weapons that the Bank of England might use in carrying out the Government's monetary policy are:

(*a*) influencing interest rates;
(*b*) open market operations;
(*c*) Special Deposits;

These are described in detail in the following sections.

WEAPONS OF THE BANK OF ENGLAND

19. Interest rates. From the early nineteenth century until 1981 the Bank of England was able to influence the level of interest rates in the money market by changing the minimum rate of interest at which it was willing to lend. The Bank led other market rates of interest by announcing its Minimum Lending Rate. (MLR) each week (this was known as Bank Rate until 1972) and other market rates followed it. Although the banks had their own base rates, to which their borrowing and lending rates were linked, they tended to move up and down with MLR. As part of the Bank of England's new monetary measures introduced in 1981 (*see* X, 5), its MLR was suspended but nevertheless the Bank has a powerful effect upon interest rates through the rates at which it buys bills in the money market.

If interest rates are raised then borrowing is discouraged and thus the credit creation process is slowed down. If interest rates are reduced then borrowing becomes more worth while and this stimulates the creation of new deposits.

20. Open market operations. These amount to the deliberate selling or buying of Treasury bills and Government stocks in order to "mop up" excess purchasing power on the one hand, or to increase purchasing power on the other. By selling securities in the open market the Government receives payment for them by cheques drawn by individuals, firms and institutions in the private sector. These cheques reduce the level of bank deposits which form the major part of the money supply. Conversely, if the Government buys securities its purchases are paid for by cheques drawn on the Bank of England and these are paid in as deposits with the commercial banking system, thus increasing the money supply.

When the Government sells securities and bank deposits are reduced so too are the cash holdings of the banks. They thus find it difficult to maintain cash and liquid assets and may have to reduce their lending which will reduce bank deposits still further. Open market operations can therefore be very effective in reducing the availability of credit to the community. Furthermore, they are used to support the Bank's measures to influence interest rates. By controlling the stock of securities available in the market it can influence their prices and hence interest rates.

21. Special Deposits. Since 1960 the Bank of England has from time to time used the device of Special Deposits in order to reduce the ability of the banks to lend by way of loans and overdrafts. A call for Special Deposits takes the form of a directive to the banks to pay over a set proportion of their eligible liabilities in cash, to be frozen as deposits with the Bank of England until such time as the bank decides to repay them. A call for, say, 2 per cent Special Deposits may cause the banks to reduce their less liquid assets (investments and advances) in order to maintain adequate liquid assets.

When Special Deposits are repaid they have the opposite effect upon the liquidity of the banks, and upon their ability to create new deposits. Although this weapon has not been used since the new measures of 1981 were introduced, it is still intended that it should be used when necessary.

22. Other weapons. Another device which a central bank can use to control credit is that of reserve assets ratios. This was used in the UK until 1981 but during the period 1971–81 it was used more as a device to ensure that the banks had adequate liquid assets than as a device to prevent them from creating credit. From 1971, when the new regulations for Competition and Credit Control came into effect, until 1981 when they were abandoned, all banking institutions had to keep, day by day, a minimum of $12\frac{1}{2}$ per cent of eligible liabilities in the form of eligible reserve assets. These assets were mainly those whose supply could be regulated by the authorities and comprised balances with the Bank of England (other than Special Deposits), commercial bills, call money with the London money market, Treasury bills, Government stocks with less than a year to maturity, local authority bills and company tax certificates.

The authorities (i.e. the Treasury and the Bank of England) could conceivably have drastically changed this 12½ per cent ratio either up or down and such a movement would of course have had an immediate effect upon the credit-creating power of the banks.

Central banks can also use directives to the banks as a weapon of control and since the Second World War, the Bank of England has made frequent use of directives to the banks and other financial institutions stipulating the action that should be taken to implement the Government's policy on bank advances.

Quantitative directives required the banks to limit the amount of their advances while qualitative directives were concerned with the type of advances, e.g. that priority must be given in lending to export industries while advances to personal borrowers must not increase. When the new arrangements for credit control were introduced in 1971, the Bank of England abandoned quantitative ceilings for bank advances but it was stipulated that the "authorities would continue to provide the banks with such qualitative guidance as may be appropriate".

The Banking Act 1979 gave the Bank of England much tighter control over the financial institutions but this is aimed primarily at ensuring that they are structurally sound rather than at pursuing its monetary policy.

We shall need to look more closely at the measures used by the Bank of England in carrying out the Government's monetary policy in X, which is devoted entirely to that subject.

PROGRESS TEST

1. When was the Bank of England established and in what way was it given preferential treatment from the outset? **(1, 2)**

2. What were the provisions of the Bank Charter Act 1844? **(3)**

3. Was the Bank of England always a central bank? **(3)**

4. When was the Bank of England nationalised and what powers was it given in the Act? **(4)**

5. What are the channels of communication between the Bank of England and the other financial institutions? **(6)**

6. What was the main purpose of the Banking Act 1979? **(5)**

7. List the functions of the Bank of England. **(7–15)**

8. What is meant by the term "lender of last resort"? **(9)**

9. Define (*a*) direct and (*b*) indirect assistance to the discount houses. **(9)**

10. Which weapons does the Bank of England use in carrying out the Government's monetary policy? **(19–22)**

11. How does the Bank of England influence interest rates? **(19)**

12. Define open market operations. **(20)**

13. What are Special Deposits? **(21)**

14. Describe the two types of directives given to the banks. **(22)**

15. Comment on the function of the Bank of England to issue and redeem Government stocks and Treasury bills. **(11, 12)**

16. How does the Bank of England operate the exchange equalisation account to stabilise exchange rates? **(14)**

17. How do the banks create credit? **(16)**

18. What is the credit-creation multiplier? **(16, 17)**

CHAPTER VII

The Evolution of Commercial Banking

DEVELOPMENTS IN THE NINETEENTH CENTURY

1. The private banks. The way in which the 400 or so small banks which existed at the turn of the nineteenth century developed from the goldsmiths has already been described (*see* III) and so too has the effect of the Bank of England's monopoly of joint-stock banking on the size of these banks (*see* VI). It is necessary now to consider the effects upon these banks of the legislation of the nineteenth century.

2. The 1826 Act. Considerable concern was expressed in Parliament in the 1820s at the growing number of failures amongst the banks, and pressure was brought to bear to abolish the Bank of England's monopoly over joint-stock banking. The banks were small institutions because they could not have more than six partners. By permitting joint-stock companies to be formed, the wealthy industrialists and land-owners could be invited to subscribe capital and enable the small banks to develop in size.

Consequently, the Country Bankers Act was passed in 1826 which permitted joint-stock banks to be established and to issue notes outside a radius of sixty-five miles from London. The radius, it was thought, would preserve the monopoly of the Bank of England within the London area, and it did in fact do so. There were no rapid developments in joint-stock banking until the restriction was relaxed in the Bank of England Act 1833.

3. The Bank of England Act 1833. This Act permitted joint-stock banking within the London area provided that the new banks did not issue their own notes. This restriction would, it was thought, restrain the growth of new London banks as note issue was considered to be essential to the expansion of banking business. This, however, overlooked the fact that "deposit banking" was becoming common. This was the term given to the practice of accepting deposits and allowing customers to borrow by drawing cheques in excess of their balances. A profit could thus be made without making loans in cash, Bank of England notes being used only for day-to-day requirements.

From then onwards, commercial banking developed rapidly. Joint-stock banks, commencing with the London County and Westminster Bank in 1836, established themselves in London and gradually the small country banks were absorbed by them to provide a network of branches throughout England and Wales. By 1841 there were 115 joint-stock banks and by the end of the nineteenth century many of these had amalgamated so that in 1914 most of the commercial banking was in the hands of the sixteen members of the London Clearing House.

DEVELOPMENTS IN THE TWENTIETH CENTURY

4. Fears of excessive power. In 1917 some of the large clearing banks began to merge and the concentration of banking into the hands of so few banks aroused such widespread apprehension that a Treasury committee was set up in 1918 to report on bank amalgamations. This committee recommended control by legislation. There was in fact no legislation but the banks agreed not to consider any further amalgamations without consulting the Treasury. The agreement worked well and although some of the smaller banks became absorbed (e.g. Coutts and District were taken over by National Provincial) there were no amalgamations of the large banks until 1968. For a long period of years prior to that date, the composition of the Clearing Banks remained unchanged as the Big Five (Barclays, Midland, Lloyds, National Provincial and Westminster, which accounted for about 80 per cent of Clearing Bank deposits), plus Coutts, District, Glyn Mills, Martins, National, and William Deacons. Of these small banks only Martins was independent.

In 1968, Barclays and Lloyds endeavoured to merge and to absorb Martins and at the same time National Provincial and Westminster announced their intention to merge. The first of these proposals was referred to the Monopolies Commission and in their case to the Commission the banks concerned contended that, quite apart from the obvious advantages that would ensue from rationalising their branches and computer systems etc., the large group would be better able to meet the needs of the very large industrial groups that had emerged and to compete with the competitive challenge of the foreign banks. In rejecting the merger proposals, but not by a very decisive majority, the Monopolies Commission was very critical of the way that the clearing banks fixed their interest rates jointly and also that, in common with the insurance companies, they did not have to disclose their true profits. Action was taken in 1969 to force the banks to show true profits and they abandoned their collective agreement on interest rates in 1971.

The Government accepted the Monopolies Commission's decision and would not allow the Barclays–Lloyds–Martins merger to take place, but it did agree that Martins could be absorbed by one of them and, in the event, Barclays took them over. The Government did permit the National Provincial/Westminster merger and also in 1970 permitted Glyn Mills, Williams Deacons and the English part of the National Bank to merge to form Williams & Glyn's Bank. Mergers among the Scottish Clearing Banks have also brought them down to three large banks (Bank of Scotland, Royal Bank of Scotland and Clydesdale). The Royal Bank of Scotland group owns Williams & Glyn's Bank and it is expected that the two banks will be fully merged in the near future under the name of Royal Bank of Scotland, to produce a large bank with 900 branches.

It is inconceivable that there will be any more mergers between what are now the Big Four banks; and the line-up of the London clearing banks is now these four (Barclays, Lloyds, Midland and National Westminster) plus Coutts and Williams & Glyn's. Coutts is wholly-owned by National Westminster. Between them the six clearing banks have some 12,000 branches and 160,000 members of staff. The Trustee Savings Bank for England and Wales, the National Girobank and the Co-operative Bank are functional members of the London Clearing House but they are not London clearing banks in the sense that the term is used in this section. There will no doubt continue to be horizontal mergers, however, between the banks and other financial institutions such as the hire-purchase finance houses, factoring houses and other houses on the fringe of banking. Recently the banks have acquired interests in stockbrokers and stockjobbers and it is quite conceivable that before the end of the century mergers between banks and building societies will take place.

5. Commercial banking. The term commercial banking has never been very clearly defined and does cause some confusion. It could be used to encompass all the banks which lie between the central bank on the one hand and the savings banks on the other and thus include the clearing banks, the merchant banks, the Trustee Savings Banks (which as we have discovered are no longer savings banks) and the National Girobank. However, the term is most frequently used to mean that type of banking carried out by the clearing banks and it is in that sense that the term is to be used throughout the rest of this book. The functions of the clearing banks are thus described in detail in later chapters and are not covered in this chapter. It is necessary, however, for us to look in detail at the functions of a merchant bank and the Trustee Savings Bank and in doing so we must inevitably compare these with those of a clearing bank.

MERCHANT BANKS

6. Accepting bills. The merchant banks originated as institutions which accepted bills of exchange on behalf of their customers. As wealthy merchants, the merchant banks had extensive connections overseas. They were highly respected and trusted and if they could be persuaded to add their names to bills of exchange then these bills became readily discountable in the London discount market at the lowest rate of interest. For merchants overseas they would agree to accept bills drawn on them up to specified limits. These became known as acceptance credits. A merchant who bought goods from a British supplier would arrange for the supplier to receive a letter from the merchant bank agreeing that the supplier should draw bills on the banker instead of on the importer. The merchant banker in effect made himself liable for the importer's debt up to a specified limit and this was very satisfactory from the exporter's point of view. This side of the merchant banker's business became very profitable and they gradually dropped their trade in commodities and became bankers. They also developed services in connection with the issuing of shares and became known as issuing houses as well as merchant banks.

In the 1960s the work of the New Issues departments developed into corporate finance. This term embraces not only bringing new companies to the market (i.e. getting their shares issued and quoted on the Stock Exchange), but also arranging takeovers and mergers, investment management and arranging syndicated loans.

The older and more influential of the merchant banks are known as accepting houses and they are members of the Accepting Houses' Association. Their accepted bills are readily discounted by the Bank of England, as are bills of all other eligible banks.

In recent years the basic distinction between a merchant bank and a clearing bank, i.e. that the merchant bank was principally engaged in lending its name through accepting bills whereas the clearing bank borrowed and lent money, has become very blurred. The merchant banks have developed the normal commercial banking services they provide and the clearing banks have increased their banking services for foreign trade very rapidly and have greatly increased their share of the acceptance business done in London. They acquired subsidiary companies or set up new ones in order to be able to bid for the large deposits that became available through the wholesale market (*see below*). Furthermore, the clearing banks have taken an increasing share of the work of issuing shares which previously was the rather sacred domain of those accepting houses which are issuing houses. A further complication lies in the fact that many of the small fringe banks that have become established in London in the last twenty years call themselves merchant banks, even though their functions are more akin to those of the clearing banks than the merchant banks. It is perhaps better to look more closely at the two main types of banking, wholesale banking and retail banking, in which both clearing and merchant banks are involved, than to pursue the possible distinctions between the two types of bank.

TRUSTEE SAVINGS BANKS

7. Reform of the banks. As we saw in V, the Page Committee recommendations of 1973 were quite dramatic in that they transformed the Trustee Savings Banks from the old concept of a savings bank to institutions that perform most of the services of the main High Street banks, though in the main only for personal customers. In 1983 a further significant change took place when the Trustee Savings Banks were amalgamated still further into two main banks, the Trustee Savings Bank for England and Wales and the Trustee Savings Bank for Scotland, plus two small banks for the Channel Islands and for Northern Ireland, and the four banks come under a holding company. Fresh legislation is expected shortly which will enable the Trustee Savings Bank(s) to go public in 1985 or 1986. The banks will then be owned by private shareholders of course in the same way as the main clearing banks, and thus be independent of the Government.

The Trustee Savings Bank for England and Wales is a functional member of the Bankers' Clearing House and is therefore able to clear cheques drawn on the London clearing banks as well as to receive from them cheques drawn on the Trustee Savings Bank. Similarly, of course, it is able to clear credit transfers.

8. Types of accounts. In the same way as the main clearing banks, the Trustee Savings Banks operate both current accounts and deposit accounts. Seven days' notice is required on normal deposit accounts on which the basic deposit rate is paid, but there are also term deposits which attract higher rates of interest depending upon the term involved and the interest may either be fixed at the outset or variable with base rate. Current account holders are issued with cheque books and cheque guarantee cards in the same way as customers of the main High Street banks and a charge may be made if a minimum balance of £100 is not maintained.

Customers of the banks can purchase and sell Stock Exchange securities through their bank. Other facilities available include the provision of foreign currency and traveller's cheques, standing orders, bankers' drafts and mail and telegraphic transfers, arrangements to make withdrawals at other banks, cash dispensers, home safes, safe custodies, insurance services, and direct transfer of wages and salaries to employees' accounts—in fact most of the personal services the main clearing banks provide. The Trustee Savings Banks also have their own unit trust.

9. Loans and overdrafts. The Trustee Savings Banks provide loans and overdrafts to their customers and inasmuch as their customers are in the main private customers their advances are mostly personal ones and include a very large amount of mortgage loans for house purchase.

10. Commercial accounts. As yet the Trustee Savings Banks have relatively few business accounts but they are increasing in number quite rapidly and the banks are developing their services to meet the needs of such customers. As yet services for importers and exporters have a considerable way to go before they can be said to match those of the main clearing banks.

WHOLESALE AND RETAIL BANKING

11. Wholesale banking. This term has arisen since the 1960s with the development of sterling inter bank lending and certificates of deposit, plus the rapid expansion of the Eurocurrency market and the local authority market in London. Very large deposits began to be deposited with the banks by other financial institutions and large companies and corporations and to change hands between the banks. The clearing banks sought to attract some of these without upsetting their existing arrangements whereby they accepted deposits at seven days' notice from their customers at a very modest rate of interest. They were able to bid for these deposits, at higher rates of interest than for seven-day deposits both directly and through subsidiary companies. At one time, in 1973, over 45 per cent of the clearing bank groups' sterling deposits were wholesale deposits, but this proportion has since dropped.

Wholesale deposits comprise deposits of £10,000 and over, received by the retail network, i.e. the banks' branches, but predominently very large deposits by other banks, institutions, and companies directly or through money brokers in the London money market, and certificates of deposit.

12. Certificates of deposit. These are documents issued acknowledging the receipt of deposits by a bank repayable to bearer against the surrender of the receipts at maturity. They are issued for larger sums of money at fixed rates of interest for fixed periods of time. The certificates of deposit (CDs) can be freely sold at any time so that, although the money is deposited for a fixed period, it is possible for the depositor to obtain cash for his asset at any time. In view of this fact the banks have been able to secure deposits on a longer-term basis than they would otherwise have been able to do.

13. Eurocurrency deposits. Eurocurrency deposits are deposits denominated in currencies other than the currency of the country in which they are deposited. For example, a deposit of US dollars with a bank in London would be a Eurodollar deposit. The vast majority of Eurocurrencies are in fact dollars, but there are several others including Eurosterling and the Euromark. The Eurodollar market emerged in the late 1950s as a result of substantial deposits of US dollars with banks in Europe by companies arising from the very large balance of payments deficits incurred by the United States.

Eurocurrencies are borrowed and lent at rates of interest that are determined by supply and demand and they form an important source of funds for the banks in London. A clearing bank or merchant bank in London receiving a deposit of a Eurocurrency is able to relend it as a Eurocurrency or alternatively switch it into sterling and use the proceeds to lend for the term of the deposit.

The majority of foreign currency deposits in London are with overseas banks with offices in the City, but the amount deposited (including certficates of deposit in foreign currencies) with the London Clearing Bank groups, i.e. including the subsidiary banks, is nevertheless very substantial indeed.

14. Retail banking. As indicated above, this term applies to the type of banking carried out by the High Street banks, and as far as deposits are concerned they are on current and deposit account. This means that they are repayable on demand (current account) or on seven days' notice. Large deposits of £10,000 or more can be used by Head Office in the wholesale money market for which the depositor receives a rate of interest higher than that payable on deposit accounts.

The ways in which these retail deposits are employed by the banks and the services provided by High Street banks is examined in Parts V, VI and VII.

OVERSEAS BANKING

15. Rapid growth in London. Since 1960, there has been a rapid increase in the number of foreign banks with offices in London and there are now over 400 of them. They have been a powerful competitive force for the London clearing banks. Many of these are American banks attracted to London by the existence of the Eurodollar market and by the desire to have a foothold in Europe.

Similarly the London clearing banks have increased their activities overseas by opening branches, especially in Europe, and by joining in with overseas banks in the establishment of consortium banks. These are banks the share capital of which is jointly owned by a number of international banks. In addition there are a number of credit unions through which British banks and their subsidiary finance houses are associated with other banks, mostly in Europe, to provide facilities for reciprocal lending. Through such an association it is possible for a British exporter to arrange for a member bank in the buyer's country to provide the credit that he needs in order to be able to pay for the goods.

PROGRESS TEST 7

1. What was the main purpose of the 1826 Act? **(2)**
2. Why was it not until after 1833 that joint-stock banks began to establish themselves in the London area? **(3)**
3. Why did the Treasury Committee in 1918 recommend control of the banks by legislation? **(4)**
4. What did the Monopolies Commission say about bank mergers in 1968? **(4)**
5. Name the London clearing banks. **(4)**
6. How did the merchant banks originate? **(6)**
7. What is meant by corporate finance? **(6)**
8. What are the distinctions between a merchant bank and a commercial bank? **(6)**
9. To what extent are the services of the Trustee Savings Bank the same as those of the main clearing banks? **(8, 9, 10)**
10. Define the terms retail banking and wholesale banking. **(11, 14)**
11. What are certificates of deposit? **(12)**
12. Explain what is meant by the term Eurocurrency. **(13)**

CHAPTER VIII

The London Discount Houses

THE LONDON MONEY MARKET

1. Definitions of the market. In its broadest sense, the money market includes the Bank of England, the clearing banks, merchant banks, other banks including foreign banks, the discount houses, the Stock Exchange, hire-purchase finance houses, assurance companies, pension funds, investment trusts and unit trusts and building societies. These are all institutions which deal in money and which through their demand for, and supply of, money, influence interest rates. These institutions, other than the discount houses, are described in other chapters.

The purpose of this chapter is to examine the activities of the discount houses and their relationships with the Bank of England and the commercial banks: all three constitute the hub of the London money market.

2. The discount houses. Within the London money market, the London discount market comprises nine major discount houses plus about the same number of smaller houses that specialise in particular fields such as dealing in bullion or as stock jobbers. The discount houses are members of the London Discount Market Association and have a unique position in that it is only to these houses that the Bank of England acts as lender of last resort.

DEVELOPMENT OF THE DISCOUNT HOUSES

3. Dealers in bills and short-term securities. Like all financial institutions, the discount houses make their profit by borrowing money and lending it at more favourable terms. They originated as institutions that would discount commercial bills of exchange. Where they were satisfied with the reputation of the parties concerned they would be prepared to pay the drawer or a subsequent holder the face value less discount and then either hold the bill until maturity or possibly resell it. Prior to the establishment of the network of branch banks in the latter part of the last century, the discount houses performed a vital role in the finance of industry and commerce through the movement of funds. Bills drawn on wealthy country landowners by the industrialists and merchants in the towns would be readily discounted. Once the banks took over the role by accepting deposits at their branches and lending money where it was required, the domestic use of bills of exchange declined and the discount houses concentrated more on the discounting of bills drawn in connection with foreign trade.

With the disruption to international trade caused by the First World War the use of foreign bills of exchange declined and the discount houses had to resort to a new form of investment. This was the Treasury bill, which was becoming increasingly used by the Government as a means of raising short-term funds. (For a description of a Treasury bill, *see* XIII, 5.) Each week the discount houses bid for all of the Treasury bill issue and all get a share, the size of which depends on how competitive their bid is in relation to other bids.

During the Second World War the Government greatly reduced its issue of Treasury bills, borrowing money direct from the banks instead against receipts given to them in exchange (Treasury deposit receipts). The discount houses then began to make a market for Government stocks nearing maturity and these formed a major part of their investment of funds until the 1960s. Since then the bill of exchange has re-emerged as the most important means of settlement of international trade. Also, a very large amount of local authorities' bonds and other securities have been issued. These have proved a popular asset with the discount houses and sterling certificates of deposit too have accounted for a large part of these loanable funds. The sources of the discount houses' borrowed funds and the way they are used as loanable funds is shown in Table IV. The difference between the total money borrowed and the total money lent indicates the use by the discount houses of their own capital funds.

Most of the money that the discount houses borrow is on a short-term basis; much of it is call money, i.e. it is lent on a day-to-day basis and can be called in by the banks at any time and at best money is lent to them on an up to fourteen days' basis. Of the total of borrowed funds in May 1983, £5,817 million (*see* Table IV), no less than £5,272 million was on a call basis. The discount houses must be careful therefore to use the funds only to acquire assets which can be readily marketed.

4. The lender of last resort. The discount houses act as a buffer between the banks and the Bank of England in that it is the houses and not the banks that have to go cap in hand to the Bank of England

TABLE IV.   LONDON DISCOUNT MARKET—SOURCES AND
USES OF BORROWED FUNDS May 1983 (£ MILLION)

Sources of funds

Borrowing in sterling from:	
UK monetary sector	5,178
other sources	502
Borrowing in other currencies from:	
UK monetary sector	109
Other sources	28
	5,817*

Uses of funds

Cash deposits with Bank of England	2
Government stocks	237
Local authority investments	159
Other investments	88
Treasury bills	114
Local authority bills	146
Other sterling bills	3,003
Sterling certificates of deposit	1,996
Funds lent to UK monetary sector	30
Loans to local authorities	143
Other loans	31
Other sterling assets	25
Currency certificates of deposit	104
Currency bills	18
Other currency assets	17
	6,063

*Of which £5,272 million was on call or overnight basis.
Source: Bank of England Bulletin

if the money market is short of funds. The Bank of England can
always inject funds into the money market if it wishes to do so by
buying bills and this it will invariably do, but the rate of interest at
which it is willing to buy bills is at times higher than the rate of interest
a discount house usually earns on the assets it acquires, and the
purpose is to force up interest rates or, at least, stop them from

falling. The activities of the Bank of England as lender of last resort are examined more fully in X.

DAY-TO-DAY TRANSACTIONS

5. Transactions with the banks. At the commencement of the day, representatives from the discount houses visit the head offices of the major banks in order to ascertain whether each individual bank is calling in any of its call money, or alternatively whether it is willing to lend any additional money. The discount houses also endeavour at the same time to sell parcels of commercial bills, Treasury bills, short-dated Government stock and other securities to the banks. They do in fact serve the banks by providing them with what they need in order to ensure that for each working day weeks ahead they hold suffcient bills and stocks to give them a steady daily flow of redemptions. There will be some negotiation of the rates of interest on any new money borrowed and on the prices at which the bills and stocks are to change hands. Much will depend upon the availability of funds in the money market at the time. When funds are plentiful interest rates will be lower than at other times when funds are scarce.

After these morning negotiations have been completed, each discount house takes stock of its position to ascertain whether it needs to borrow more or whether it has surplus funds. During the day it will endeavour to rectify whichever of these situations it finds itself in in order to balance its books. It must borrow if it is short of funds and it will not wish to have any funds that are not invested by the end of the day. Telephone calls will be made to the banks and other financial institutions and as a last resort it will go to the Bank of England.

6. Direct and indirect assistance. The Bank of England will help the discount houses that are short of funds by either direct or indirect assistance. Direct assistance involves buying bills from them, while in order to give indirect assistance the Bank of England will buy the bills from the banks to enable them to increase their call money loans to the discount houses. The choice of direct or indirect assistance is a matter of tactics and rests very much with the Bank of England.

7. Securities. During the day the discount houses must send round to the banks the parcels of bills and other securities they agreed to sell to them during the early morning negotiations. They must also put up parcels of bills and stocks as security for any additional loans negotiated during the day.

PROGRESS TEST 8

1. Which institutions constitute the London money market? **(1)**

2. Briefly describe the history and development of the discount houses. **(3)**

3. Name the main sources from which the discount houses obtain their funds. **(3)**

4. Describe the purposes of the daily visits of the discount houses to the banks. **(5)**

5. Define (*a*) direct and (*b*) indirect assistance. **(6)**

6. For what purposes do parcels of bills and other securities pass between the discount houses and the banks? **(7)**

CHAPTER IX

Money Market Interrelationships

THE STOCK EXCHANGE

1. Market for stocks and shares. Through the London Stock Exchange investors are able to buy and sell stocks and shares. Public companies are able to apply to the Stock Exchange Council for their shares to be quoted and if this is agreed there will be both a buying and a selling price quoted for those shares and this will be determined by the demand for, and the supply of, the shares. If there are any irregularities in the conduct of the company's affairs concerning such matters as takeover bids or dealings in its shares, the quotation may be discontinued.

The dealers in this particular market (the Stock Exchange) consist of stockbrokers and stockjobbers. The brokers act as agents between the investor and the stockjobber and receive a fixed scale of commission for the service. The jobbers deal in particular types of stocks or shares, e.g. motor shares, and trade on their own account and do not come into contact with the investing public. They buy shares from one stockbroker and sell them to another, taking as their profit the difference between the buying price and the selling price. Share quotations are double-barrelled, i.e. two prices are given such as 96p–99p, the former being the jobber's buying price and the latter his selling price. Contracts between jobbers are agreed verbally and followed later by written contracts. Payments for Government stocks are made as soon as the broker's client receives a contract note but payments in respect of company shares are due on settlement day, normally about ten days after the end of the account period which lasts for two weeks. Completion of the transfer of ownership of the stocks and shares is done by the registrar of the company concerned who issues a share certificate to the new owner indicating his name and address. This is not necessary for bearer securities, of course, which simply pass from one person to another without registration of their names.

2. New issues. New issues of shares are made on behalf of the companies concerned by the issuing houses (the merchant banks) and by the issue departments of the clearing banks. They offer shares to the investing public by way of a published prospectus in the national press or to the institutional investors such as the assurance companies. The issues are underwritten by both the issuing houses and / or the other financial institutions involved. This means that if all the shares are not taken up they undertake to buy the remainder. Underwriters who have taken up shares then sell them on the Stock Exchange after dealings in the new shares begin.

3. Government broker. One of the firms of stockbrokers in London is the Government's broker and, acting under instructions from the Bank of England, will buy and sell Government stocks. The Bank of England invites applications for new stocks from the public (mostly responded to by the institutions) but also will always have a tap stock in the hands of the Government broker. This term is applied to the latest issue of stock which has yet to be completely taken up by investors and it is derived from the fact that the Government broker turns on the tap and makes more of the stock available on the market when it is expedient to do so. The clearing banks, merchant banks, overseas banks, discount houses, investment trusts and unit trusts, insurance companies, pension funds and all the other institutions in the City of London are thus able to build up their portfolios of Government stocks and, if necessary, to dispose of some of them through the Stock Exchange. Similarly, these institutions are able to buy and sell shares through the Stock Exchange and the New Issues Market.

OTHER RELATIONSHIPS

4. Government buyer. In the same way that the Government broker acts on behalf of the Bank of England in the Stock Exchange, so a London discount house acts as the Government buyer in the London discount market. This discount house is used by the Bank when it wants to make extra funds available or, more usually, in order to mop up surplus funds by selling additional Treasury bills and other securities. Through the Government buyer and the Government broker the Bank of England is able to influence interest rates in the short-term and long-term money markets respectively.

5. Banks and other institutions. The banks maintain accounts for some of the other financial institutions and offer normal facilities, especially the payments mechanisms of both cheques and credit transfers. Without the banks the building societies, insurance companies, investment trusts, hire-purchase finance houses etc.

would find it very difficult to function. Their receipts of cash and cheques are paid into the banks and their loans and investments are carried out by drawing cheques on their accounts with the banks. To some extent the banks are involved in another way with some of these institutions in that they hold shares in them or may own them completely as subsidiary companies.

6. Parallel markets. From what has been covered by this and the previous two chapters, it will be clear to the reader that the London money market has become increasingly complex in recent years and that new types of market have arisen. These are sometimes referred to as "parallel markets" meaning that they run parallel to the London discount market. These markets are the inter-bank market through which very large deposits pass from bank to bank; the certificates of deposit market (*see* VII, **12**); the local authority market through which local authorities have been able to borrow on a short-term basis; and the Eurocurrency market (*see* VII, **13**). In addition the hire-purchase finance houses have developed their services and are much more involved in the provision of finance for industry than they were twenty years ago. There has also been some swapping of surplus funds between some of the larger companies, i.e. an inter-company market.

Money and deposit brokers act between these various parallel markets, bringing about switches of funds from one market to another as interest rates fluctuate, and bringing about a relationship in interest rates in the London money market in its widest sense.

PROGRESS TEST 9

1. How are the prices of stocks and shares determined?　**(1)**
2. What is the difference between a stockbroker and a stock-jobber?　**(1)**
3. Explain how share prices are quoted.　**(1)**
4. When do payments have to be made for stocks and shares?　**(1)**
5. What is meant by underwriting a share issue?　**(2)**
6. Explain the role of the Government broker.　**(3)**
7. What is the function of the Government buyer?　**(4)**
8. Explain the relationship between the banks and other institutions as banker and customer.　**(5)**
9. Which are the parallel markets?　**(6)**
10. What is the function of money and deposit brokers?　**(6)**

CHAPTER X

Monetary Policy

REGULATING DEMAND

1. The purpose of monetary policy. The main objective of monetary policy is to control the amount of the money supply and both the cost and the availability of credit, in order to regulate demand in an endeavour to control the rate of inflation and achieve a high rate of economic growth with a low rate of unemployment.

A government's monetary policy must be part of its economic strategy as a whole because it is little use adopting a particular monetary policy if its fiscal policy and maybe direct controls, such as an incomes policy, are pulling in the opposite direction. It is particularly important that the government should be adopting a restrictive fiscal policy (the policy concerned with its own income and expenditure), if at the same time it is endeavouring to restrain the rate of increase in the money supply.

It is not always possible for a government to achieve all of its objectives, of course, and quite often they conflict with one another. For instance, in order to control inflation a restrictive monetary policy may be necessary which involves a high level of interest rates and restrictions on bank credit, but in order to achieve this objective of low inflation the level of economic activity may fall and unemployment rise. Quite often, too, external factors, such as a high level of interest rates in other countries, may make it impossible for a government to pursue the monetary policy it wishes.

In the UK the responsibility for carrying out the government's monetary policy is shared by the Treasury and the Bank of England, jointly known as "the authorities". The weapons which the Bank of England uses were considered in Chapter VI and the appropriate parts of that chapter should be read in conjunction with the present chapter.

2. The quantity theory of money. There is undoubtedly some connection between the general level of prices and the quantity of money and various attempts have been made to assess how close this connection is. The original Quantity Theory of Money still has a ring of truth about it but it is far too simplistic a theory for it to be of much use in measuring what is likely to happen to prices if the money supply is increased at a particular rate. The theory is that the money stock multiplied by its velocity of circulation must equal the general level of prices times the number of transactions. This can be expressed by the equation of exchange as follows:

$$MV = PT$$

where M = money supply
V = velocity of circulation
P = prices
T = transactions.

The velocity of circulation is the number of times money changes hands in a given period and this is very difficult to measure with any degree of accuracy. It is possible to obtain a very crude measure of the extent to which the velocity of circulation of part of the money supply, viz. bank deposits, has changed, by comparing the value of cheques passing through the London Clearing House, as a proportion of the total of bank deposits, with a similar proportion for the previous year. But this is a very crude measure in that the Clearing House figures are distorted by the very large payments that pass between the various financial institutions in the City which have little to do with the velocity of circulation of money within the community in respect of transactions in goods and services. But in any case it is not possible to measure the velocity of circulation of notes and coin which form the remainder of the money supply.

If we could measure the velocity of circulation and it could be shown that V is independent of M, then any increase in M must result in an increase in either P or T or both. As T is likely to remain unchanged in the short period then an increase in M would result in an increase in P. Obviously, then, the theory is a weak one unless it can be related to reality in a more convincing way. Later economists attempted to do this by adopting an incomes approach. They used a new equation:

$$Y = kM$$

where Y = money income of the community
M = money stock
k = the average number of times each unit of money is received as income.

Here the velocity is rather different from the velocity of circulation of money in the broad sense in which it is used in the equation of exchange. We are now concerned with the proportion of total income which the community wishes to hold in money form, which determines the size of k, and if this proportion remains stable we then have a reliable link between money and income. If, assuming no change in k, the money supply is increased while the national income remains static, prices will rise. Only if there are under-used resources is national income likely to rise quickly enough for the increase in the money supply to be required to maintain the ratio k, and therefore it is not very likely that an increase in the money stock will in itself trigger off an increase in the national income.

The value of k may change, of course, and this is likely to happen during a period of severe inflation when holders of money might decide to hold less of it and buy goods as a hedge against inflation. At such a time the extra spending would stimulate production so that Y would increase and therefore the existing money stock would still be required to achieve the new proportion of income to be held as money (k). If production does not rise under such circumstances, prices will rise still further and stimulate the tendency to buy goods rather than hold money.

If, when the money stock increases, the community decides to buy more to restore k to what it was previously, and they spend the money in acquiring financial assets such as stocks and shares, the demand for these assets will force up their prices and therefore the yields on them will decline. There is therefore a link between the money stock and interest rates, and the higher the level of interest rates the greater will be the attractiveness of financial assets, thus reducing the demand for money to hold (k). There is also a link between interest rates and the level of capital investment so that there is thus an indirect link between capital investment and the size of the money stock.

From what we have been considering it is clear that the money supply is a very useful target for the Government's economic policy, but opinions differ as to the extent to which a Government should use this target. The "monetarists" would of course claim that this is the best target of all to use, while those who favour more direct controls on the economy would wish to see control of the money supply employed in a rather neutral fashion.

Besides control of the money stock there are a number of other monetary variables which can be used, such as control of bank credit, interest rates, exchange rates and direct controls over the level of expenditure.

THE PRICE OF MONEY

3. Interest rates. In Chapter VI we considered the ways in which the

Bank of England has sought to influence the level of interest rates through Bank Rate, then M.L.R. and, more recently, through its unpublished interest rate bands at which it is prepared to buy bills in the money market. We now need to look more closely at the use of the interest-rate weapon as a device for pursuing a particular monetary policy.

The purpose of either directly controlling or influencing the level of interest rates is either to make money dearer or to make it cheaper. If money is made dearer then borrowing is discouraged and this reduces the creation of credit, i.e. reduces that rate of increase in the money supply. If interest rates are reduced and money is made cheaper then borrowing is encouraged, which will increase the supply of credit, which in turn increases the money supply. The Bank of England must endeavour to attain the level of interest rates that will bring forth that amount of bank lending which would bring the money stock up to the desired level. This assumes that the private sector of the community will respond in the expected way to a change in the price of money. However, this may not always happen because other factors, such as the future prospects for profits and the level of inflation, will also affect the desire to borrow. There is also likely to be a time lag between the raising or lowering of interest rates and the respective reduction or increase in the level of borrowing, because it takes time to reduce spending commitments or to acquire new capital equipment and stocks.

There may at times be conflict between the use of interest rates domestically and externally. When, for instance, it has been desirable to reduce interest rates in order to expand the economy by encouraging borrowing and expenditure, especially capital expenditure, it has at the same time been necessary to avoid an outflow of capital attracted by higher interest rates abroad. This makes the use of the interest rate weapon very difficult from time to time and attempts are frequently made to achieve a concerted interest rates policy by the major countries of the world. It is particularly necessary for the United States to be pursuing a similar interest rates policy to that of countries such as the UK at any particular time, if low interest rates are to be used as a stimulus to economic growth. It is also necessary for a government to make its interest rates effective by its open-market operations.

4. Open-market operations. In order to make its interest rate policy effective the central bank must use open market operations. When the central bank sells bills in the market to institutions in the private sector it reduces their balances with it. To restore these balances, the banks in particular may have to squeeze the discount house by calling in call money, and thus the discount houses are forced to seek finance from the Bank of England. In other countries the banks would be obliged as a last restort to seek finance themselves from the central bank. When the central bank is approached as the last resort it is able to impose higher rates of interest if it wishes to do so. In the UK the Bank of England usually gives assistance to the discount houses by offering to buy bills, and it was for this reason that, as part of the new monetary measures in 1981, it increased the number of banks whose bills would be eligible for rediscounting at the Bank (the *eligible banks*). When bills are offered for rediscounting at the Bank of England the Bank will refuse to buy them unless the price at which they are offered is in accord with their interest rate bands, which they alone know. If a discount house is seeking too high a price for its bills and thus in effect demanding finance at too low a rate of interest, the Bank will decline to buy and it is then up to the discount house to make a fresh offer to the Bank which may be more acceptable.

In a country where the banks are obliged to keep a minimum reserve ratio the central bank may also use open-market operations in order to reduce (or increase) the availability of liquid assets in the market and thus make it difficult for the banks to maintain their reserve ratio. If they find it difficult to do so they may be obliged to reduce the level of their advances in order to increase their cash balances.

THE 1981 MEASURES

5. Existing UK monetary controls. The monetary control measures introduced by the Bank of England in 1981 removed the "corset" whereby the banks were from time to time penalised if they increased their interest-bearing deposits by more than a target amount. For any excess, they had been obliged to pay over supplementary special deposits to the Bank of England on which no interest was paid, which was indeed a high penalty as it was these particular deposits on which they were paying a high rate of interest in order to attract them. The measures also involved the abolition of the $12\frac{1}{2}$ per cent reserve assets ratio which the banks had been obliged to maintain since 1971 when the Competition and Credit Control regulations were enforced, and, further, the removal of the requirement that they should keep at least $1\frac{1}{2}$ per cent of their eligible liabilities in balances at the Bank of England. Although Minimum Lending Rate (M.L.R.) was not abolished by the 1981 measures, it is no longer published, but the Bank of England reserves the right to reintroduce it at any time. Instead of M.L.R. the Bank now has a number of interest rate bands, which are not published, and within which it will be prepared to rediscount bills for the discount houses, and it is through the rediscounting of bills at rates agreeable to itself that the main tenet of the Bank of England's 1981 measures lies.

Apart from the use of the Bank of England's "discount window" in this way, to a much greater extent than before, the other 1981 measures are that all of the banks and licensed deposit-takers must now maintain a non-operational account at the Bank of England which amounts to ½ per cent of their eligible liabilities, and that the banks must hold at least 2½ per cent of the eligible liabilities in secured loans to the discount houses each day. In addition they must maintain these loans to the discount houses and certain other specialised intermediaries at a level of at least 5 per cent on a daily average basis over six months or a year. This is to ensure that the discount market has sufficient funds to buy bills in order to maintain a large bills market for the Bank of England to carry out its open-market operations in. Quite apart from its desire to enforce its interest rates policy, the Bank of England uses its day-to-day intervention in the money market to even out the flow of funds between the public sector and the private sector, and vice versa. Each day the banks inform the Bank of England what balances they require in order to meet their commitments for the day, and by combining this knowledge with its own information about flows of funds between the banks and the public sector, the Bank of England is able to estimate the likely shortage (or surplus) of funds in the money market. It announces this estimate in the morning and revises it at midday if necessary.

6. Balance of payments and monetary policy. When the balance of payments is adverse the Government may decide to tackle the problem by dampening down the demand for goods and services, and hence the demand for imports, by using its monetary controls, and, as we have seen, in the UK the government would now rely primarily on the use of interest rates to bring this about. However, there is the alternative of letting the exchange rate take the strain and this can be easily achieved with floating exchange rates. Say, for instance, the exchange rate between the US dollar and sterling stands at $1.5000 = £1 and the UK balance of payments is in deficit; then, if the exchange rate is allowed to fall to, say, $1.3000 = £1, British goods will become much cheaper to the American buyer and thus our exports will be stimulated. At the same time our imports would become dearer because a UK importer will receive less dollars for every pound, and this will discourage imports. In theory the exchange rate between the dollar and sterling will settle down at a rate at which there will be equilibrium between payments to the US and payments to the UK, and of course a similar situation will exist with the rate of exchange between sterling and each other foreign currency. In reality the situation is not as simple as this, because of economic factors other than trade between countries and also because of political factors, but nevertheless exchange rates can play an important part in putting right a balance of payments deficit. By relying on exchange rates to put the balance of payments right a country is then in a better position to use its monetary controls in order to achieve other objectives such as economic growth and a higher level of employment.

PROGRESS TEST 10

1. What are the purposes of monetary policy? **(1)**

2. In the UK who is responsible for carrying out the government's monetary policy? **(1)**

3. Explain the quantity theory of money and illustrate it with the equation of exchange. **(2)**

4. Define the incomes approach to the quantity theory of money. **(2)**

5. Besides the control of the money stock what other monetary variables are there? **(2)**

6. What is the purpose of controlling the level of interest rates? **(3)**

7. How might the use of interest rates internally and externally conflict? **(3)**

8. How does the Bank of England use open-market operations to support its interest rates policy? **(4)**

9. What are the existing UK monetary controls? **(5)**

10. How might exchange rates be used to put a balance of payments deficit right? **(6)**

PART FOUR

THE LEGAL BACKGROUND

CHAPTER XI

Relationship with Customers

DUTIES AND RESPONSIBILITIES

1. Contractual relationship. Usually no written contract exists between a bank and its customer apart, possibly, from a mandate giving signing instructions if there is more than one party to the account or it is an account for a corporate body. There is however a verbal agreement or understanding giving an implied contract based on the rights and duties of both bank and customer as established by banking practice and case law. This contract is between debtor and creditor and at times between principal and agent, and it has changed over the years as banking practice has changed.

It is important that a bank in carrying out its services, particularly that of collecting a cheque, should do so *for a customer*. This is made clear in s.4 Cheques Act 1957, for instance, which states that when collecting a cheque the bank must receive payment for a customer. As to what consitutes a customer it is necessary to rely on case law. In *Great Western Railway* v. *London and County Banking Co.* (1901) it was held that a customer must have a current account or a deposit account or *some similar relationship*. This has been taken to mean that where a "customer" does not have an account but, for instance, deposits valuables on safe custody or receives investment advice, he is a customer in the legal sense. Case law has also established that a continuous relationship is not essential to the definition of a customer and that the relationship exists immediately an account is opened and money paid into it (*Ladbroke and Co.* v. *Todd* (1914) and *Commissioners of Taxation* v. *English, Scottish and Australian Bank* (.920)).

Case law has also laid it down that a bank must take up references when opening an account. It may open the account on a conditional basis, it being understood that if the references are unsatisfactory the account will be closed.

2. Basic duties of banker and customer. The duties of a banker were examined in *Joachimson* v. *Swiss Bank Corporation* (1921) and were stated to be that:

(*a*) The banker must receive money from and collect cheques and other bills of exchange for the customer and repay the money against the customer's written order. The order must be addressed to the branch where the account is kept and repayment made at that branch during named working hours.

(*b*) The bank must give reasonable notice before closing an account in order that the customer may make other arrangements and also so that any cheques that may have been drawn may reach the bank.

This judgment established the unusual principle that, as far as the banker–customer relationship is concerned, the debtor must seek out the creditor.

As far as the customer is concerned, his written order, i.e. his cheque, must be drawn with reasonable care whether he writes the cheque himself or delegates the task to someone else. This was established in the case of *London Joint Stock Bank* v. *Macmillan and Arthur* (1918) in which an employee had written out a cheque but did not insert the amount in words and left a space either side of the figure for the amount and the employer signed it. The employee then increased the amount of the cheque by inserting figures on either side of the original figure and inserted the new amount in words. It was held that the customer did not excercise reasonable care and the judgment went against him. As far as the banker's responsibilities when paying his customer's cheques and when collecting cheques for him are concerned, we shall need to examine these in detail in the context of negotiable instruments in XII.

The banker has an implied right to charge interest on a loan or overdraft, to make reasonable charges for his services, and to be reimbursed for expenses incurred in acting on behalf of the customer. He also has the right to repayment on demand of any advance and has a right of lien over property lodged with the bank other than on safe custody (*see* XV).

As agent for the customer the bank acts in vicarious capacity and must obey his principal's instructions with reasonable competence and diligence. He must render an account to his principal when it is required, must avoid placing himself in a position where his own interest would clash with that of the customer (the principal), and must not make any secret profit over and above the commission he charges. The banker must also keep the customer's affairs secret.

3. Secrecy. Generally speaking a bank must not divulge information about its customer's affairs and this is an age-old principle which is rigidly observed. However, there are some occasions when disclosure without the customer's consent may be justified and these were clearly categorised in the case of *Tournier* v. *National Provincial Bank* (1924) as follows:

(*a*) *Under compulsion of law.* If a court directs a bank to produce a customer's statement of account. (Subsequent enactments have compelled banks to disclose the amount of deposit interest paid to customers beyond a minimum amount in submitting returns to the Inland Revenue. Furthermore, where an inspector is investigating the affairs of a company he may require information from a bank.)

(*b*) *Duty to the public.* Where the customer is known to be doing something which is vitally against the national interest.

(*c*) *In the interests of the bank.* For instance, where the bank is demanding payment from a guarantor of the amount outstanding and needs to inform him of the amount of the customer's debt.

(*d*) *Where the customer's interest demands disclosure.* A good example of this is where the bank replies to a status enquiry concerning a customer, which it has an implied authority to do. Also, where the bank is dealing with the manager of a business and there is an implied consent for the bank to disclose information to him.

4. Status reports. A bank has an implied consent to answer status enquiries concerning a customer received from another bank or credit reference agency and has express authority where the customer has given the bank's name as a reference or instructs the bank to answer such an enquiry. However, the bank must be careful in the wording of its reply if it is to avoid the risk of breach of contract or of being sued for libel or slander for a remark of a defamatory nature. The banks do not divulge the balance on a customer's account and give only a general answer from which the enquirer can make his own deductions. They must, however, show their customers in a true light.

The banks do not sign status reports and they always include a disclaimer of reponsibility and mention the fact that they are not a credit-reporting agency under the Consumer Credit Act 1974, under which credit agencies may be forced to disclose their opinion.

As far as claims of fraud or negligence are concerned, the former could not succeed if the report was unsigned and the latter could only succeed if it could be established that the bank had some contractual or fiduciary relationship with the enquirer.

5. Safe custodies. Banks must take adequate care of boxes and parcels, stocks and shares and other items lodged with them for safe custody or they may be sued for negligence. The bank is the *bailee* and the customer the *bailor* of such property. A gratuitous bailee must take *reasonable* care while a paid bailee must take the *maximum possible* care. However, the distinction between the two types of bailee is now of less importance in that the banks all take very good care of property, using up-to-date security devices, and therefore they now usually charge for the service. Banks require boxes to be locked and parcels to be sealed before they take them on safe custody and on their receipt they usually state that the contents are unknown. They also advise the customer to take out insurance against loss. In these ways a bank may possibly succeed in reducing any claims against it for loss or damage.

If a bank hands over an item on safe custody to someone who is not the rightful owner it may be sued for *conversion*, which is an unauthorised act which deprives another person of his property.

TYPES OF CUSTOMER

6. Minors. A minor is a person under 18 years of age. He or she is not bound by contracts, cannot give a guarantee, nor borrow against a guarantee. Normally a bank will insist that the account of a minor is kept in credit because of its inability to enforce repayment. However, they do use their discretion in this matter and will lend to minors on occasions where, for instance, a parent who is well known to the bank vouches for the son or daughter's overdraft.

A minor may be a party to a joint account, but would not be liable in respect of any overdraft incurred while he was a minor. He may also be a partner and operate on the partnership account. He may incur an overdraft as agent for the partnership but he is not personally liable until he reaches his majority, apart from his share of the partnership assets in the event of bankruptcy of the partnership.

7. Married women. A married woman may operate a bank account, borrow money and pledge security, and use all the banking services in the same way as a married man, or for that matter, a single man or woman. If she is a minor she is treated as any other minor as far as opening and running an account is concerned.

The bank will require the usual references when opening the account and, as for a man, will want to know the occupation and the name of her employer. The bank may also require to know the name of her husband and of his employer in view of the decision in *Savory and Co.* v. *Lloyds Bank* (1932) in which the bank was found negligent in not making these enquiries when opening a wife's account.

When a married woman deposits security on behalf of another person, especially her husband, the bank usually arranges for her to be independently advised by a solicitor.

8. Joint accounts. When a joint account is opened the parties to it are required to sign a mandate form in which they indicate which of the account holders are to sign on the account and to withdraw any items lodged as security with the bank. The form also establishes *joint and several liability* in respect of any borrowing on the account, so that in the event of legal action to recover the debt the bank can sue the parties to the account jointly and then each party individually until the whole debt is recovered. The bank has a right of set-off between the private accounts of the individual parties and their joint account.

When a party to a joint account dies the normal procedure for dealing with the estate within the terms of his or her will, or within the rules relating to survivorship if there is not a will, applies. However, this is for the suriving parties to a joint account to sort out for themselves and, as far as the bank is concerned, it could get a good discharge by paying over the credit balance on a joint account to the surviving parties or by taking a new mandate on the account signed by them. As far as safe custodies are concerned, the banks usually hand them over against the signatures of the surviving parties plus the executors or administrators of the deceased's estate.

In the event of bankruptcy of one of the parties to a joint account, the account must be stopped and the balance and any safe custodies released only against the signatures of the solvent parties plus that of the trustee or official receiver. Should the account be overdrawn the security of the bankrupt party will continue to be held unless the remaining parties repay the overdraft or undertake to do so. A rather similar situation applies where a party to an account becomes mentally incapable, but instead of requiring the signature of the trustee or official receiver in each instance, that of the Court of Protection is required.

9. Club accounts. A club or society is a non-profit making association which has no separate entity. The members are not responsible for any borrowing unless they agree to be, in which case the banks would probably require a personal guarantee.

The bank's mandate for the account refers to a meeting of the club at which it was resolved that the account should be opened and that specified persons should sign on the account. The bank will usually wish to have a copy of the club's rules.

10. Executors and administrators. The personal representatives of a deceased person will open an account in their names, followed by an indication that they are the executors or administrators of the person concerned. Normal references are required if they are not already known to the bank. If there is a will the persons named in the will to act for the deceased are executors, and their powers to act are confirmed by *probate* which is an official copy of the will and certificate that it has been proved. If there is no will or the named executors are not willing to act, then persons willing to settle the estate must apply to be appointed by court as administrators of the estate. If appointed they receive letters of administration.

The executors or administrators must present these official documents to the deceased's bank in order to withdraw the credit balance on his account and to take possession of any securities on safe custody. If there is an overdraft on the deceased's account the personal representatives may elect to pay it off in order to obtain possession of securities or the bank may agree to release the securities in order that they may be sold off in order to repay the advance. Frequently the banks are asked to advance money to executors and to administrators to pay capital transfer tax which must be settled with the Inland Revenue before probate or letters of administration will be granted.

11. Sole traders. A person in business on his own may simply have a bank account in his own name through which all the firm's transactions are passed. Alternatively, if he is trading under a business name the account may be opened in his name followed by 'Trading as......'

He is entirely responsible for the firm's affairs and will be required to provide his own security for any advance required by the business.

12. Partnership accounts. A partnership is defined in the Partnership Act 1890 as "the relation which subsists between persons carrying on business in common with a view to profit". There must not be more than 20 partners unless the partnership is of practising solicitors or accountants or of persons carrying on business on the Stock Exchange. There need not be any written partnership agreement but if there is not then the provisions laid down in the Partnership Act as to responsibilities of partners apply.

It is not necessary for the business name of a partnership (or of a sole trader) to be registered, but the names of the partners must appear on the firm's notepaper and other business documents and they must be displayed at the firm's premises. A bank must satisfy itself that the persons opening the account are the true partners.

A partnership is not a separate entity, as is a company, and therefore all the partners are jointly liable for all of the firm's activities including any borrowing. The bank will therefore require a mandate which gives joint and several liability. In a trading firm there is an implied authority for any partner to bind the firm in respect of bills of exchange, promissory notes, contracts of borrowing and any pledge or sale of the firm's assets except in transactions under seal. In a non-trading firm, a partner cannot bind the firm in respect of these items, apart from cheques, unless they are part of the firm's usual business. A partner cannot without express authority bind the firm by deed nor execute a guarantee in the firm's name, unless giving guarantees forms part of the firm's normal business. It is therefore necessary for a bank to obtain the signatures of all partners to a guarantee.

Upon the death of a partner a credit account may continue but a new mandate is required. If the partnership account is overdrawn a claim may have to be lodged against the deceased partner's estate, and therefore the account should be stopped and a new account opened for the remaining partners.

13. Company accounts. A company is a legal person and has rights and responsibilities quite separate from its shareholders. The majority of companies are incorporated and registered with the Registrar of Companies under the Companies Acts 1948–81, but there are a few that have been set up by Royal Charter or as nationalised corporations.

Most companies are *limited companies* in which the liability of the members is limited to the amount of the shares they hold or of the guarantee they have given. However, there are some unlimited companies in which the members are fully liable for the company's debts without limit.

A company may be a *private company* or a *public company*. A private company may not offer its shares to the general public whereas a public company may do so. There is no limit as to the number of members for either type of company, but private companies still tend to restrict their membership; with both types there must be a minimum of two members.

Companies, whether public or private, must register the following documents with the Registrar of Companies:

(*a*) Memorandum of association.

(*b*) Articles of association.

(*c*) A statement giving the names of directors and of the secretary, and accompanied by their written consents to act. Included in the statement must be the address of the registered office.

(*d*) A declaration of compliance with the Companies Act 1948 concerning registration.

(*e*) A statement of the company's capital, if there is any.

The memorandum of association is the company's charter with the general public, and the company can act only within the powers laid down in it. The memorandum contains the name of the registered office of the company. The name must end with the word Limited (Ltd) if it is a private company, and Public Limited Company (plc) if it is a public company (or the Welsh equivalents). In addition, the objects of the company must be given, the company's powers, the fact that liability is to be limited, and the authorised capital of the company.

The objects clause must give details of the purpose for which the company has been formed. If any transaction entered into by the company exceeds those authorised in the objects clause, it may be *ultra vires* (beyond the powers) and such an act cannot be rectified by members of the company. However, the European Communities Act 1972 provides that anyone dealing with a company can enforce an *ultra vires* contract against it if he dealt in good faith and if the transaction was decided on by the directors. The same act stipulated that a third party may assume that the powers of the directors to bind the company are not limited under the memorandum and articles of association, that he need not enquire as to the capacity of the company to enter into the transaction or about the powers of the directors. He is presumed to have acted in good faith unless it can be proved that the contrary is the case. However, it is doubtful whether a bank could claim protection under these provisions in that it would receive a copy of the memorandum and articles when the account was opened. The company's powers, such as to borrow money and acquire businesses, will usually be listed in addition to its objects.

The articles of association are concerned with the company's relationship with its members such as the rights of shareholders to vote at company meetings, the issue and transfer of shares, the powers of directors and conduct of meetings.

A certificate of incorporation brings a company into existence and is issued by the Registrar of Companies only when he is satisfied with the documents filed. In addition to the certificate of incorporation a public company requires a trading certificate before it can commence trading, and it must satisfy the Registrar that its share capital requirements have been completed before this will be issued. A public company may also wish to apply to the Stock Exchange Council for its shares to be quoted on the Stock Exchange.

When a bank opens an account for a company it will need to see all the documents listed above and must be careful not to lend money to the company until the trading certificate has been seen. The bank will keep copies of the memorandum and articles of association and will require a certified copy of a resolution appointing the first directors of the company unless they are named in the articles. The bank's mandate will have to be signed by the chairman and secretary of the company referring to the meeting of the board of directors at which the resolution contained in the mandate was passed. The mandate will indicate the signatories on the account. Cheques and other instruments must be signed "for and on behalf of" or "per pro" the company and each signature must be followed by an indication of the person's capacity in the company.

AGENCY

14. Acts by agents. We have already examined in this chapter the role of the bank as agent for its customer and it is now necessary for us to consider how a bank is affected by its customer appointing an agent to act for him and by the customer himself acting as agent for some other person.

Where a customer appoints someone to act as his agent in running his account the bank will want to see the authority in writing before it will act upon it even though a principal may appoint an agent by word of mouth. Usually the bank's form will be signed by the customer listing the powers of the agent, but the bank may be willing to act upon a general power of attorney. The bank will want to be introduced to the agent and will require a specimen signature. The agent is responsible to his principal, the bank's customer, for his actions and must act within his powers. The bank must know what these powers are and make sure they are not exceeded because the principal is not bound by the agent's actions if they exceed these powers.

When signing cheques and other documents on behalf of the customer, the agent must do so by procuration, i.e. sign "per pro". As far as cheques and other bills of exchange are concerned, this is covered by s. 25 Bills of Exchange Act which states that by procuration operates as notice that the agent has but limited authority to sign, and the principal is only bound by such signature if the agent in so signing was acting within the actual limits of his authority.

If an agent exceeds the authority in borrowing money from the bank, the bank cannot enforce repayment unless the principal agrees, or is in some way unable to deny the agent's lack of authority. This is particularly important in the context of borrowing by directors of a company.

Where the bank's customer acts as agent for some other person the bank is not greatly affected; however the bank may be put on enquiry if the customer draws cheques on the principal's account and pays them into his own (*Midland Bank* v. *Reckitt and Others* (1933)). Where the customer is agent to the bank as principal the bank is of course greatly affected by the agent's actions. Such a situation exists where, for instance, the bank is lending money to its customer against goods imported by him for which the bank holds the shipping documents. The bank might under these circumstances be willing to let the customer handle the documents as the bank's agent in order that he may gain access to the goods to resell them. The documents are released against a trust receipt which clearly establishes that the customer is to act as the bank's agent.

In sending bills of exchange for collection and in opening documentary credits the banks use banks abroad as agents and are responsible for these agents' actions. They are to some extent protected against the negligence or unauthorised acts by the *Uniform Rules for Collections and the Uniform Customs and Practice for Documentary Credits* (*see* XVIII).

PROGRESS TEST 11

1. What two types of contract may exist between bank and customer? **(1)**

2. What constitutes a customer of a bank? **(1)**

3. What are the basic duties of a banker as laid down in *Joachimson* v. *Swiss Bank Corporation* (1921)? **(2)**

4. When a customer draws a cheque why must he act with reasonable care? **(2)**

5. What are the banker's responsibilities when he acts in a vicarious capacity for his customer? **(2)**

6. Under what circumstances may a bank divulge information about its customer's affairs? **(3)**

7. If a bank is bound by a bond of secrecy why is it that it will be prepared to answer a status enquiry concerning its customer? **(4)**

8. What is meant by conversion? **(5)**

9. What are a banker's responsibilities as bailor of his customer's property? **(5)**

10. Is it permissible for a minor to run a bank account and, if so, may he overdraw it? **(6)**

11. When a married woman opens an account what information is the bank likely to require and why? **(7)**

12. What will be contained in the mandate taken by a bank when opening a joint account? **(8)**

13. Under what circumstances may a club account be overdrawn? **(9)**

14. What is the difference between an executor and an administrator? Is a bank likely to lend money to such personal representatives? **(10)**

15. On what basis is a sole trader's account usually operated **(11)**

16. When a bank opens an account for a partnership what type of mandate will it require and what information will be necessary? **(12,**

17. What is the difference between a private company and a public company? **(13)**

18. What information is to be found in the memorandum and articles of association respectively? **(13)**

19. In the bank's mandate in respect of a company's account what information is to be found? **(13)**

20. How are the banks affected by the acts of agents? **(14)**

CHAPTER XII

Banking Instruments

BILLS OF EXCHANGE

1. The concept of negotiability. Negotiability is a term used in relation to instruments used to transfer money such as cheques and other bills of exchange, promissory notes, dividend warrants, bearer bonds and Treasury bills, all of which are known as negotiable instruments.

When a negotiable instrument is transferred to another person the person receiving it has a good title to it even if a previous holder had a bad title. However, this assumes that the recipient was unaware that a previous holder had a bad title and that the recipient was acting in good faith. Negotiable instruments are therefore very different from items which are not negotiable, such as goods and chattels, in that the purchaser of a good cannot get a better title to it than a previous owner and therefore if it had been stolen the rightful owner might claim repossession even if the purchaser was quite unaware of the theft and was acting in good faith.

A negotiable instrument has the following features:

(*a*) It can be transferred by simple delivery or, if it is payable to order, by indorsement and delivery.

(*b*) It can be sued on by the person to whom it is negotiated in his own name.

(*c*) Provided the instrument is in good and regular order, the person to whom it is negotiated obtains a good title to it. However, it must be taken in good faith and for value without any knowledge of defect in the title of the transferor.

(*d*) There is no need to give notice of transfer to the person liable on the instrument, i.e. the drawer. The drawer of a bill of exchange (including a cheque) promises that it will be paid when it is presented to the person or bank on whom it is drawn at the appropriate place and time.

The fact that an instrument such as a cheque is negotiable makes it more acceptable as a means of payment in that the person accepting it does not need to worry about the rights of previous holders provided that he has no reason to be suspicious.

The subject of negotiability is covered by the Bills of Exchange Act 1882 as amended and extended by the Cheques Act 1957. Negotiable instruments are *choses in action*, which means that they are property the right to which is enforceable in a court of law.

2. Origin of bills of exchange. The bill of exchange has been used as a method of payment in Britain for six centuries or more. It originated as a convenient way of giving someone a period of credit, and thus time to re-sell the goods before paying, and at the same time providing a document that was evidence of a debt. If someone, whether he was a goldsmith, a banker or a private wealthy individual, was willing to buy the document at a discount, then the drawer of the bill could get immediate finance rather than have to wait until the bill was paid. The bill was an alternative to notes and coin as a method of payment and was used fairly extensively as an internal means of payment until the cheque came into its own in the nineteenth century, since when the bill of exchange, although still very important for international payments, has had a more limited use domestically but even in respect of transactions within Britain its importance must not be underestimated. For example, there are some trades where the bill of exchange remains a useful device for financing the dealer, e.g. motor distributors and radio and television dealers, and in some cases hire-purchase finance houses allow bills to be drawn on them as a means whereby the dealer can obtain funds with which to stock his showrooms.

Internationally the Bill on London has always been regarded as a sound means of payment. If the overseas exporter to Britain was able to draw a bill of exchange on a firm or bank in London of international repute and get the bill accepted, then he was quite happy to supply the goods and await payment. Several of the British companies who were well known in particular parts of the world as traders found that the acceptance of bills drawn on them in this way became a profitable sideline. They could sell this service to British importers who were less well known than themselves, i.e. they would accept bills on behalf of the British importer drawn on them by foreign suppliers and would charge the importer a commission for doing this. These commissions encouraged them to hive off their merchanting business and establish accepting houses, later to be known as merchant banks (*see* VII).

3. Definition of a bill. A bill of exchange is defined in the Bills of Exchange Act 1882 as follows: "An unconditional order in writing, addressed by one person to another, signed by the person giving it; requiring the person to whom it is addressed to pay on demand or at a fixed or determinable future time a sum certain in money to, or to the order of, a specified person, or to bearer."

A cheque is defined in the Act as a bill of exchange drawn on a banker payable on demand. If we bear these two facts in mind we can look at the official definition of a bill of exchange in further detail and use it to cover both a cheque and a bill of exchange.

Firstly, *a bill must be unconditional.* This means that the drawer must not stipulate some action which must be performed before the bill (or cheque) is paid, such as "provided my house has been satisfactorily painted". Clearly it would be impossible for a banker to cope with cheques that had such clauses written into them.

The *bill must be in writing.* The term writing includes printing and typewriting. The 1882 Act does not state that it must be written on paper and in consequence there have been instances in which cheques have been drawn on other materials, even on the back of a cow, and paid.

Addressed by one person to another means legal "person" to include such legal entities as companies and institutions. In fact, as we have already seen, a cheque must be drawn on a bank.

A bill of exchange *must be signed by the drawer* and therefore a bill or cheque is not valid unless it is signed.

A cheque must be *payable on demand* but other bills of exchange *may be payable on demand or at a fixed or determinable future time.* If it is payable in the future it is a *usance* or *term* bill. A bill which is stated to be payable on 1st July is payable at a fixed date, whereas one which is payable, say, 2 months (or maybe 60 days) after date or sight is payable at a determinable future date. The date of maturity of a bill payable so many days or months after date is calculated from the date of the bill, whereas on one which is payable so many days or months after sight it is calculated from the date it is sighted by the drawee, which is usually the date on which the bill is accepted by him. Where a bill is payable a set number of months after date or sight it is payable on the day of the month on which the bill is dated or sighted but no allowance is made for days lacking in the month. Thus a 3 months bill dated 15th May is payable on 15th August but one drawn on 30th November would be payable on 28th February (29th if it is a leap year). The maturity date of a bill that is payable a set number of days after date or sight must be worked out precisely. For example, a 90 days bill dated 17th July would be payable on 15th October calculated on the following basis:

14 days left in July
31 days in August
30 days in September
15 days in October

___

90

___

The sum in the bill must be certain but it may include interest, be
stated by instalments, or be stated by instalments with a provision
that upon default the whole sum shall become due. The sum can also
be calculable at an indicated rate of exchange, or according to a rate
of exchange to be ascertained as described by the bill. Where there is a
discrepancy between the amount in words and the amount in figures
the amount in words is the amount payable but it is usual practice in
such circumstances for a bank to return a cheque unpaid with the
comment "words and figures differ".

A bill may be made *payable to, or to the order of, a specified person
or to bearer*. Usually cheques have the words "or order" printed on
them and in any case the payee can make a bill or cheque payable to
his order by indorsing it on the back and writing above his signature
an instruction to pay a particular person. A bill may be made payable
to two or more persons jointly or to one or some of several payees. A
bearer bill is one payable to bearer or is one that is indorsed in blank
or one that is payable to a fictitious person.

4. Acceptance, indorsement and discharge of a bill. A bill of
exchange has to be accepted by the drawee before he is legally liable
on the bill. His acceptance must be written on the bill and signed by
him as his assent to the order of the drawer. *Cheques and promissory
notes do not require acceptance.* Usually the acceptor writes
"Accepted" or "Accepted payable at . . . . . ." across the face of the bill
but his mere signature is sufficient (s. 17 Bills of Exchange Act). An
acceptance may be general or qualified. A qualified acceptance may,
for instance, stipulate acceptance subject to fulfilment of a condition
stated in the acceptance, or it may specify that payment will be made
only at a specified place, or it may undertake to pay only part of the
amount.

The term *indorsement* (aternative spelling *endorsement*) means the
signature of the payee or of an indorsee on the back of a bill, cheque
or promissory note. The act of indorsement is necessary when such an
instrument is negotiated unless the instrument is payable to bearer.
When an instrument is indorsed and delivered to a person, i.e. it is

negotiated, he becomes the legal holder of it and he receives such title as the transferor had in it. Where the payee or indorsee is wrongly designated or his name is misspelt, he may indorse as described, adding if he wishes his proper signature.

An indorsement in blank is a straightforward signature of the payee or indorsee, whereas a special indorsement has an instruction to pay to a specified person above the payee's or indorsee's signature. The person who indorses an instrument is the *indorser* and the person to whom it is specially indorsed is the *indorsee*. Where an indorsement is in blank a holder may convert it into a special indorsement by writing above the indorsement a direction to pay the bill to, or to the order of, himself or some other person.

The need for indorsement of cheques, as distinct from bills and promissory notes, was greatly reduced by the Cheques Act 1957 (*see* **13** *below*).

A bill of exchange is discharged by payment in due course by or on behalf of the drawee or acceptor. The term *payment in due course* means payment made at or after the maturity of the bill to the holder of it in good faith and without notice that his title to the bill is defective.

A bill is also discharged if:

(*a*) the acceptor is or becomes the holder at or after maturity in his own right;

(*b*) the holder unconditionally renounces any right against the acceptor in writing or by delivering up the bill to the acceptor;

(*c*) the holder (or his agent) intentionally cancels the bill by indicating this on it.

(*d*) it is an accommodation bill (*see below*), when it is paid in due course by the party accommodated.

The liability of any party to a bill may be renounced by the holder by notice of renunciation, or the party may be discharged by the intentional cancellation of the holder's signature. In such a case, any indorser who would have had a right of recourse against the party whose signature is cancelled is also discharged.

An *accommodation bill* is one drawn on and accepted by a person in order to provide temporary finance for the drawer. The drawer may then be able to discount the bill (i.e. sell it) at the face value less discount, and make use of the money until the maturity of the bill.

5. Alteration to a bill. A bill must not be materially altered without the approval of all the parties to it. A material alteration is to the date, the sum payable, the time of payment, the place of payment, and where the bill has been accepted generally, the addition of a place of payment without the acceptor's assent. Where such an alteration is made to a bill the bill is not valid except against a party who has personally made, authorised, or consented to the alteration, and subsequent indorsers. However, where an alteration is not apparent a subsequent holder in due course may use the bill as if it had not been altered.

6. The holder of a bill. The payee or indorsee of a bill who is in possession of it, or the bearer of a bearer bill, is the holder of the bill within the definition given in the Bills of Exchange Act. The holder could be an unlawful holder or someone who has obtained the bill by fraud.

A holder of a bill may be a *holder for value,* i.e. a holder of a bill for which value has at any time been given. He is holder for value as regards the acceptor and all parties to the bill who became parties prior to the time that value was given. Value means any consideration sufficient to support a simple contract or an antecedent debt or liability.

A holder may also be a *holder in due course,* which is a holder who has taken a bill complete and regular on the face of it before it was overdue and without notice that it had previously been dishonoured, if such was the fact. He must also have taken the bill in good faith and for value and at the time the bill was negotiated he must have had no notice of any defect in the title of the person who negotiated it.

The phrase *complete and regular on the face of it* means that the bill is properly dated and signed, with no discrepancy as to the amount, and the indorsement(s) must be in order. The phrase *no defect in title* means that neither the bill nor the acceptance on it was obtained by fraud, duress, force or fear, or other unlawful means, or for an illegal consideration, nor that the bill was negotiated in breach of faith or under such circumstances as amount to a fraud.

Every holder of a bill is prima facie deemed to be a holder in due course, and such a holder has the maximum possible protection in a court of law. It is up to the person taking an action to prove that the holder of the bill is not a holder in due course.

7. Parties to a bill. Apart from the drawer and the drawee, there are two other parties who are liable on a bill as signatories to it; they are the acceptor (who most likely will be the drawee) and any indorser. The signatures of all of these parties must be genuine (s. 24 Bills of Exchange Act) and in order to be liable on a bill the drawer or indorser must deliver it, which means that there must be an actual or constructive transfer of possession of the bill from one person to another. The drawer, acceptor or indorser must have the capacity to contract, for example must not be a minor, and must receive consideration.

The *drawer* of a bill engages that on due presentation it will be accepted and paid and that if it is dishonoured he will compensate the holder or any indorser who is compelled to pay it, provided that the requisite proceedings on dishonour are taken. He cannot deny to a holder in due course the payee's existence or capacity to indorse the bill. The drawer is principal debtor on the bill until it is accepted and if it is negotiated any indorsers incur secondary liability as surety for payment by the drawer.

The *drawee* is liable on the bill once he has accepted it, when he engages that he will pay it according to the tenor of his acceptance. He is precluded from denying to a holder in due course the existence of the drawer, the genuineness of his signature, and his capacity and authority to draw the bill. Where the bill is payable to the drawer's order, the drawee cannot deny the drawer's capacity to indorse, but this does not include the genuineness or validity of the indorsement. Nor where a bill is payable to a third person can the drawee deny the existence of the payee and his capacity to indorse, but this does not include the genuineness or validity of the indorsement.

By his acceptance, the *acceptor* becomes the principal debtor and the drawer and indorsees become surities for payment by the acceptor.

An *indorser* of a bill promises that the bill will be duly accepted and paid and that if it is dishonoured he will compensate the holder or a subsequent indorser who is compelled to pay it, provided that the requisite proceedings on dishonour are duly taken. An indorser is precluded from denying to a holder in due course the genuineness and regularity of the drawer's signature and all previous indorsements and from denying to the immediate or subsequent indorsee that the bill was at the time of indorsement a valid and subsisting bill, and that he had a good title to the bill.

8. Procedure on dishonour. When a bill of exchange is dishonoured by non-acceptance or non-payment, notice of dishonour must be given without delay to the drawer and any indorsers, otherwise they are discharged from liability. Notice can be dispensed with if the person to whom it is given cannot be found, or it has been waived. A dishonoured inland bill need not be noted or protested by the holder in order to preserve the recourse against the drawer or indorser, but a foreign bill must be protested for non-acceptance or non-payment, as appropriate, otherwise the drawer and indorsers are discharged. *Noting* is the process whereby a notary public re-presents the bill for acceptance or payment and if it is dishonoured the reply is noted on the bill. If a notary public is not available the process may be carried out by a householder in front of two witnesses. The next stage in the process is the formal *protesting* of the bill. A protest is a document which contains a copy of the bill and a declaration by the notary public of the facts concerning the dishonour. The noting and protest are evidence which can be used in a court of law when taking action against the acceptor, or, if necessary, the drawer and indorsers.

9. Bills and the banker. A banker may well be the drawee and/or acceptor of a bill and in the case of a cheque he will always be the drawee. Therefore all that has been said so far in this chapter concerning the rights and duties of the parties to a bill apply equally well to the banker. In addition, both the Bills of Exchange Act and the Cheques Act provide special protection to the banker in both the collection and payment of bills, but as the vast majority of bills handled by the banks are in fact cheques this special protection will be looked at further on in this chapter in the context of the banks' handling of cheques.

CHEQUES

10. Origin of the cheque. In III we examined the emergence of bank deposits as the major part of the money supply. In this connection the cheque had a very important part to play and we now need to examine the origin of the cheque and its uses as a means of payment.

Cheques owe their origin to the practice by wealthy bank account holders of writing notes to their banks instructing them to pay cash to a particular person (possibly a manservant) to obviate the need to appear personally at the bank in order to draw out cash. This convenient practice quickly spread and the banks issued special forms (cheques) for the convenience of customers. This device was used not only to enable a third person to draw cash from a bank on behalf of the account holder, but to settle a debt with a third person who could if he wished pass it on to someone else in payment of a debt, instead of presenting it to the bank for payment. The ultimate holder of the cheque was not obliged to take cash for it when he presented it to the bank for payment and might simply pay it into his account. The use of cheques developed together with the postal system and communications generally. The amalgamation of the banks into a small group of them with branch networks was also taking place and this too accelerated the use of cheques. It became less necessary to pass a cheque from hand to hand as it became easier to get to a bank to pay it in. Furthermore the banks established a clearing system whereby they could collect the proceeds for customers of cheques drawn on other banks.

In the twentieth century the use of cheques has been greatly stimulated by increasing affluence which has encouraged the use of bank accounts. Another factor has been the Wages Act 1960 which legalised the payment of wages by cheque, if the employee agrees, and the introduction of the cheque guarantee card has made payment for goods by cheque acceptable to shopkeepers. More recently the widespread installation of automated teller machines, which enable bank customers to obtain cash after the banks are closed, has made it more convenient to workers to have their salaries and wages credited direct to bank accounts and thus to make use of the cheque system.

11. Parties to a cheque. Figure 1 illustrates a cheque. In this example the parties to the cheque are F. C. Wood, the drawer (the bank's customer), Metropolitan Bank Ltd, the drawee, and S. Hendy, the payee (the person who is to receive payment).

This particular cheque is an order cheque. This means that S. Hendy can order that the value of the cheque be paid to another person specified by him. He does this by indorsing the cheque, "Pay John Allder or order", and signing his name below this indorsement. A bearer cheque is simply made payable to "bearer" and can be presented for payment by anyone in possession of it. Obviously it is risky to make out a cheque in this way for if it is stolen the proceeds may be paid over to a person who is not entitled to the money. The vast majority of cheques are therefore order cheques.

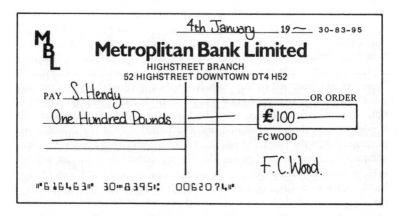

FIG. 1   *A Cheque.*

12. Crossed cheques. A cheque, such as that in Fig. 1, which has two parallel lines drawn across the face of it is a crossed cheque. The effect of this crossing is that the cheque cannot be cashed across the counter, i.e. it must be paid into a bank account. If a banker pays a crossed cheque to anyone other than another banker he is liable to the true owner of the cheque for any loss he may sustain owing to the cheque having been so paid (s. 79 Bills of Exchange Act 1882). The crossing does not have to be printed on the cheque; it can be added in ink by the drawer, the payee or any subsequent holder. A bank customer may elect to have a book of cheques that are not crossed, because the majority of his cheques are drawn for the withdrawal of cash and when he does pay a third party by cheque he crosses it in ink. Alternatively, a customer who uses his cheque book in the main for payments to third parties would be wise to ask for crossed cheques and to "open" any cheques that are used for withdrawing cash. This can be done by writing "Pay cash" between the crossing on the cheque and adding his signature. This is quite contrary to s. 78 Bills of Exchange Act 1882 which says that it is not lawful for anyone to obliterate, to add or to alter a crossing. However, although there is no legal protection for a banker who accepts such an alteration to a crossing, it is hardly likely that the customer is going to take the banker to court for obeying his instruction and, in fact, it is becoming common practice not to require customers to "open" cheques for cash in which case, of course, the paying bank is contravening s. 79. The banker would only cash such a cheque for the drawer himself or his known agent, of course.

The crossing on a cheque may be general or specific. A general crossing means that it is simply crossed with two parallel lines, with or without the addition of the words "& Co." or "and company". This addition has no real significance and is gradually fading into disuse. Where a cheque bears a specific crossing the name of a bank is written between the two parallel lines or may simply be written or stamped across the face of the cheque without the lines. Such a crossing means that the cheque must be paid only to the bank stated on the crossing. Quite often a specific crossing mentions the name of the account into which the cheque is to be paid as well as the name of the bank. This information is quite often impressed by rubber stamp by the company or institution receiving the cheque and clearly this is for security reasons as a banker would be guilty of negligence if he allowed such a cheque to be paid into an account other than that mentioned in the crossing, for instance into the account of an employee of the company.

The Bills of Exchange Act is quite specific as to who may cross a cheque, as follows:

(*a*) A cheque may be crossed generally or specially by the drawer

(*b*) Where a cheque is uncrossed, the holder may cross it generally or specially.

(*c*) Where a cheque is crossed generally, the holder may cross it specially.

(*d*) Where a cheque is crossed generally or specially, the holder may add the words "not negotiable".

(*e*) Where a cheque is crossed specially, the banker to whom it is crossed may again across it specially to another banker for collection.

(*f*) Where an uncrossed cheque, or a cheque crossed generally, is sent to a banker for collection, the banker may also cross it specially to the bank itself.

A crossing is a material part of a cheque and it is not lawful for anyone to obliterate or add to or alter a crossing except as specified above.

Sometimes the words "Account Payee" are written between the crossing on a cheque, but they have no statutory significance. A cheque bearing such words can still be negotiated or transferred, and the paying banker is not affected by the restriction. However, the collecting banker might be considered negligent if he collected such a cheque for a person other than the payee without seeking a satisfactory explanation from the person paying it in.

13. Indorsement of cheques. Until 1957 it was necessary for a cheque other than one payable to "cash" or to "bearer" to be indorsed by the payee or by the person to whom he made it payable, before it was paid. With such an enormous quantity of cheques passing through the banking system it had by then become an overwhelming task to check that all cheques were properly indorsed when they were paid in or presented for payment at the counter.

The Cheques Act 1957 abolished the requirement (contained in the Bills of Exchange Act 1882) for cheques to be indorsed, where they are paid in for the credit of the account of the payee. The actual wording of s. 1 of the Act is "Where a banker in good faith and in the ordinary course of business pays a cheque drawn on him which is not indorsed or is irregularly indorsed, he does not, in doing so, incur any liability by reason only of the absence of, or irregularity in, indorsement, and he is deemed to have paid it in due course". This went well beyond what had been recommended, which was to abolish the need for indorsement where a cheque is paid by its payee into his account. However, the Act does say "in the ordinary course of business" and to make clear what they regarded by the term the Committee of London Clearing Bankers published a list of instruments which still require indorsement as follows:

(a) Order cheques which are paid into an account other than that of the payee.

(b) Cheques presented for encashment at the counter other than those made payable to Cash or Wages.

(c) Bills of Exchange (i.e. other than cheques).

(d) Combined cheques and receipt forms marked "R".

(e) Travellers' cheques.

(f) Promissory notes.

Where a cheque bears a receipt form on the back and the cheque is marked "R" on the face, both the collecting and the paying banks must check that the receipt form has been signed. Generally, the receipt forms on the back of cheques which used to serve both for the indorsement and for a receipt specifically required by such drawers as insurance companies, are now rather unnecessary. The 1957 Act specified that an unindorsed cheque which appears to have been paid by the banker on whom it is drawn is evidence of the receipt by the payee of the sum payable by the cheque.

14. The paying banker. The banker who pays his customer's cheque "in due course" is protected by s. 59 Bills of Exchange Act. "In due course" means payment made at or after the maturity of a bill of exchange (including a cheque of course) to the holder in good faith and without notice that the title to the bill is defective. The banker is also protected by s. 60 when he pays a cheque which bears a forged or unauthorised indorsement provided he pays it in good faith and in the ordinary course of business, but of course the Cheques Act 1957 largely removes the need for indorsement anyway. If the banker knew that an indorsement was forged he would not be acting in good faith, and to pay a cheque in the ordinary course of business he would have to do so during normal banking hours and within normal banking practice. Further protection is provided for the paying banker by s. 80 Bills of Exchange Act which states that if he pays a crossed cheque to a banker in good faith and without negligence he is placed in the same position as if payment had been made to the true owner of the cheque.

The paying banker must pay his customer's cheque provided it is properly drawn and there are sufficient funds on the account or arrangements have been made for an overdraft which covers the amount of the cheque. However the cheque must not be stale or post-dated, nor must there be any legal barrier to payment.

A stale cheque is one which has been in circulation for a lengthy period of time and generally this is construed by the banks as six months. If a cheque is post-dated it must not be paid until on or after the due date and the customer would be quite within his rights to stop such a cheque before that due date. There is of course also the danger that he may die or become bankrupt before the due date.

The legal barriers to payment are the customer's death, his mental incapacity, notice of his bankruptcy, a receiving or winding-up order against him, a garnishee order or a court injunction. A garnishee order is obtained by a creditor who has a judgement against his debtor. It orders the debtor's bank to pay over the balance on his account to the creditor. A court injunction might be served on a bank where there is some dispute concerning the ownership of funds on the account. The injunction prevents the bank from making further payments from the account until the dispute is settled.

A banker must not pay a cheque which has been materially altered, as we have seen (**5** *above*) or one which has been stopped by him or one on which the customer's signature is forged. If he does pay such a cheque he is liable for damages to the customer. Such damages could be very substantial if it could be shown that the banker was guilty of libel as well as breach of contract. If a cheque is to be returned through lack of funds the banker will therefore be very careful when stating the reason for its dishonour and usually uses the wording "Refer to Drawer" which, despite the implication, cannot be considered libellous.

A banker could be liable to the true owner of a cheque for conversion should he pay it to a person not entitled to it. However, as a paying banker is unlikely to know whether the presenter of a cheque has a good title to it, he is given a great deal of protection by ss. 59, 60 and 80 Bills of Exchange Act and s. 1 Cheques Act.

15. The collecting banker. A collecting banker may also be liable for conversion by collecting a cheque on behalf of a customer who has no title to it, but he too is given some protection by both s. 90 Bills of Exchange Act and s. 4 Cheques Act. The former protects a banker who collects a cheque for a customer in good faith. This means that the collection must be done honestly and with reasonable care following the usual banking practice. In the case of *Marfani and Co.* v. *Midland Bank* (1968) it was held that as banking practice changes over the years cases decided years ago might not be a reliable guide to what the duty of a careful banker is today. The courts should examine current banking practice and decide whether it meets the standard of care required from a prudent banker. The Cheques Act (s. 4) protects a banker who collects payment of a cheque in good faith and without negligence and stipulates that the banker is not negligent by reason only of failure to be concerned with the absence of (or irregularity in) an indorsement of a cheque.

As to what constitutes negligence on the part of a collecting banker, the courts have been quite specific at various times, as shown by the following examples:

(*a*) Failure to obtain the name of the customer's employers (*Savory and Co.* v. *Lloyds Bank* (1932)).

(*b*) Failure to obtain references in respect of a new customer who was not known to the bank (*Ladbroke and Co.* v. *Todd* (1914), and failure to check on the authenticity of a reference (*Guardians of St John's Hampstead* v. *Barclays Bank (1923)* and *Lumsden and Co.* v. *London Trustee Savings Bank* (1971)).

(*c*) Collecting a cheque for an official of a company, i.e. paid into his private account (*Underwood* v. *Bank of Liverpool and Martins Bank* (1924) and *Orbit Mining and Trading Co.* v. *Westminster Bank* (1963)).

(*d*) Collecting for an agent's private account cheques payable to him in his capacity as agent, or cheques drawn by him as an attorney (*Marquess of Bute* v. *Barclays Bank* (1955) and *Midland Bank* v. *Reckitt and Others* (1933)).

(*e*) Collecting for a company's account cheques payable to another company (*London and Montrose Shipbuilding and Repairing Co.* v. *Barclays Bank* (1926)).

(*f*) Collecting cheques inconsistent with the customer's business or private activities (*Nu-Stilo Footwear* v. *Lloyds Bank* (1956)).

(*g*) Collecting third-party cheques without appropriate enquiries:

(*i*) where customer's account has been unsatisfactory (*Motor Traders Guarantee Corporation Ltd* v. *Midland Bank* (1937);

(*ii*) cheques marked "Account Payee" (*House Property Co. of London and Others* v. *London County and Westminster Bank* (1915));

(*iii*) where circumstances warrant enquiry—cheques payable to partnership (*Baker* v. *Barclays Bank* (1955)).

If a banker can show that he has given value for a cheque and is therefore collecting it in his own right and not as agent for the customer he may be able to claim protection as a holder in due course in any action for conversion. This might arise where he cashes a third party cheque for a customer or cashes a cheque for a customer of another bank or branch and there is no open credit arrangement. This would also be the case where he has allowed a customer to draw against a cheque before it is cleared or where he takes a cheque in specific reduction of an overdraft or where he has a lien on a cheque which has been returned unpaid and to debit the customer's account would cause it to be overdrawn.

PROMISSORY NOTES

16. Definition. The Bills of Exchange Act 1882 defines a promissory note as: "an unconditional promise in writing made by one person to another, signed by the maker, engaging to pay, on demand or at a fixed or determinable future time, a sum certain in money, to, or to the order of, a specified person or to bearer."

This is in effect an IOU in that it is a promise to pay a sum of money; but an IOU is not a negotiable instrument whereas a promissory note is, nor does an IOU state the date on which payment is to be made. The reader will notice the similarity of wording between this definition and that of a bill of exchange, the main difference being that one is a promise to pay (and thus it emanates from the person who owes the money) while the other (the bill) is an order to pay (and is drawn by the person to whom the debt is due).

The most common form of promissory note is the bank-note issued by the Bank of England which carries the wording, "I promise to pay the bearer on demand the sum of five pounds" (or whatever denomination it is). Promissory notes, other than bank-notes, are rarely used for commercial transactions these days, apart from some capital goods contracts in international trade. As promissory notes are negotiable instruments their title is transferred by delivery to the payee or to bearer.

PROGRESS TEST 12

1. What is meant by the term negotiability? **(1)**
2. Explain how bills of exchange originated and why it was that they became less popular as an internal means of payment in the nineteenth century. **(2)**
3. What is meant by the Bill on London? **(2)**
4. Give the official definition of a bill of exchange. In which Act is it to be found? **(3)**
5. What is a usance bill? **(3)**
6. From what date is the maturity of a bill payable at three months after sight calculated? **(3)**
7. How does the drawee of a bill of exchange accept the bill? **(4)**
8. When is it necessary for a bill of exchange to be indorsed? **(4, 13)**
9. Distinguish between a general indorsement and a special indorsement. **(4)**

10. What is meant by the term "payment in due course"? **(4)**

11. What is an accommodation bill? **(4)**

12. What is meant by the material alteration of a bill? **(5)**

13. Who is a holder in due course of a bill? **(6)**

14. What does the drawer of a bill undertake when he draws it? **(7)**

15. Describe the responsibilities of the acceptor of a bill. **(7)**

16. What does an indorser promise when he indorses a bill? **(7)**

17. Explain the procedure when a bill is dishonoured. **(8)**

18. Do the rights and duties of the parties to a bill apply to a banker? **(9)**

19. Explain how the cheque originated. **(10)**

20. Define a cheque and explain the difference, if any, between this definition and that of a bill of exchange. **(13)**

21. Distinguish between an order cheque and a bearer cheque. **(11)**

22. What is the purpose of crossing a cheque? **(12)**

23. Who may cross a cheque? **(12)**

24. Does a cheque serve as a receipt? **(13)**

25. In what ways is a paying banker protected by law? **(14)**

26. When must a banker refuse to pay a cheque? **(14)**

27. Is a collecting banker protected by law? **(15)**

28. Under what circumstance might a collecting banker be considered negligent? **(15)**

29. Under what circumstance might a collecting banker be able to claim protection as a holder in due course? **(15)**

30. Define a promissory note and distinguish it from a bill of exchange. **(16)**

PART FIVE

COMMERCIAL BANKS' SOURCES AND USES OF FUNDS

CHAPTER XIII

Profitability v. Liquidity

BANK BALANCE SHEETS

1. Simplified balance sheet. A simplified balance sheet of one of the large banking groups is illustrated in Fig. 2. This is intended to demonstrate the main assets and liabilities of a bank and how the two must be related in order to satisfy the bank's shareholders on the one hand and the account holders on the other. The shareholders will expect the bank to make as big a profit as possible whereas the customers will expect the bank to keep sufficient liquid assets to be able to repay deposits when required.

These two requirements are rather conflicting, in that the more liquid an asset is the less will it earn in interest, and vice versa, so that the bank must draw a very careful balance between them. To some extent, this task is taken out of the bank's hands if a minimum reserve ratio in approved liquid assets is laid down, but there is nevertheless quite a lot of room for the bank to manoeuvre.

The two aspects of profitability and liquidity can best be considered by looking at each of the assets in turn, and this is done in the following sections.

2. A bank's liabilities. In common with all public and private companies, the banking groups have shareholders and they keep reserves. Hence the first liability shown on the balance sheet is "capital and reserves". The size of this item is very small in comparison with the total of the balance sheet (only about 5 per cent of total liabilities) whereas with other types of trading companies the major part of the total is due to the shareholders and they in effect own the assets between them. In addition to shareholders' funds the banking group is likely to have borrowed capital, i.e. loan capital as indicated in the simplified balance sheet.

A bank, and indeed any institution which borrows and lends money, has another and much larger liability, this is to those persons and firms who have deposited money with the bank, i.e. the depositors, and the majority of the assets represent the investment of the depositors' funds and only to a modest extent the shareholders'

Liabilities	£ million	Assets	£ million
Capital & reserves	2,500	Cash and balances with central banks	700
		Money at call and short notice	8,000
Loan capital	1,000	Treasury bills	200
		Other bills	500
		Dealing assets	200
Deposits	50,000	Cheques in course for collection	1,000
		Certificates of deposit	700
		Investments,	1,000
		Advances	40,000
		Trade investment	20
		Investments in associated companies	180
		Premises	1,000
	53,500		53,500

FIG. 2 *Simplified balance sheet of a banking group.*

capital. The term deposits is used in a general sense to mean all deposits whether on current account or deposit account and includes funds "purchased" in the wholesale money markets. The ratio of current accounts to deposit accounts has varied considerably and depends a great deal upon the level of interest rates. When interest rates are high account holders tend to transfer some of their current account balances to deposit accounts. As we progress down the balance sheet, we will find that the most liquid assets are at the top and the least liquid assets at the bottom; the least profitable are at the top and the most profitable at the bottom.

3. Cash. Turning to the "assets" side, the item which is loosely called "cash" consists not only of notes and coin actually held by the bank but also the current account balance at the Bank of England and the compulsory deposit of ½ per cent on the special non-operational account. The current account is as good as cash in that at any time the bank can withdraw in notes and coin from the Bank of England and will in fact on every working day be paying in old notes for destruction and surplus notes and coin and obtaining its requirements in new and usable notes and in coin. Until 1971, the banks maintained a minimum cash ratio of 8 per cent, i.e. the total of cash, including the balance at the Bank of England, expressed as a proportion of total deposits. This proportion was considered to be unnecessarily high for the bank's day-to-day needs, especially as the other liquid assets could easily be converted into cash if required, and since then they have maintained a much smaller amount of cash. In Fig. 2 it will be seen that the ratio of cash to deposits is only about 1½ per cent. As cash (both in the tills and at the Bank of England) earns no income, it is understandable that the banks would want to keep as little of it as possible.

4. Money at call and short notice. The next most liquid asset is money at call. This is money that is lent to the discount houses and to other borrowers, the vast majority of it on an overnight basis and the rest for periods of up to fourteen days. Most of it is lent to the discount houses and the remainder to money brokers, discount brokers, jobbers and stockbrokers and bullion brokers. The rates of interest charged on call money vary with the length of the loan, overnight loans attracting a lower rate than loans for a week; and they also depend upon the availability of funds in the market. When money is plentiful on a particular day new loans will attract only a low rate of interest, whereas on days when funds are short the rate will be considerably higher.

5. Treasury bills. These are bills of ninety-one days' tenor issued by the Treasury either on a tap or on a tender basis. Tap bills are issued and sold in the market to suit the convenience of the Treasury, i.e. the Bank of England "turns on the tap". Tender bills, on the other hand, are put up for tender each Friday, would-be bidders being informed a week in advance of the amount of bills (possibly £150—£200 million) that will be on offer on the following Friday. The discount houses bid for the whole amount in accordance with a "gentleman's agreement" with the Government. The Government is thus assured of the money that it needs to borrow in this way and, in exchange, the Bank of

England undertakes to act as a lender of last resort to the discount houses.

Other institutions, such as the overseas banks and the commercial banks (on behalf of customers), tender for bills in competition with the discount houses and to the extent that they succeed in outbidding them, receive an allocation of bills. The commercial banks also have a "gentleman's agreement" with the discount houses to the effect that they will not compete in the tender on their own accounts as a *quid pro quo* for the convenience of having the discount houses act as a buffer between them and the Bank of England. When there is a shortage of funds in the money market it is the discount houses and not the banks that are forced to obtain funds from the Bank of England by rediscounting bills, possibly at a penal rate of interest. The banks obtain their requirements of Treasury bills by buying them from the discount houses, usually after they have been held for at least a month.

The rate of interest on Treasury bills is determined by the gap between their nominal value and the actual price paid. For each £100 of Treasury bills (this is notional as the smallest bill is £5,000) a bid of, say, £97.25 may be made. The bidder is thus prepared to pay over £97.25 immediately for £100 in ninety-one day's time. The annual rate of interest is therefore approximately £2.75 × 4 = 11 per cent. In reality, this is worked out very precisely because ninety-one days is not exactly a quarter of a year and the money lent is £97.25 not £100. The bid price will depend upon the rates of interest that the discount houses are having to pay for the funds that they borrow, but usually the average rate of interest on Treasury bills is about ½—1 per cent below the banks' base rate.

6. Other bills. These are bank bills, local authority bills, and commercial bills which the bank has discounted and which it holds till maturity. The yield to the bank on these, i.e. the rate of interest at which it has discounted them, varies with the length of time to maturity and will range from about ½ per cent above the bank's base rate to 1½ per cent above.

7. Dealing assets. This item consists of Government stocks and other investments held for the purpose dealing in the money markets and as such are liquid assets.

8. Cheques in course of collection and balances with other banks. This represents the total of cheques and other items that have been sent to the London Clearing House for collection and balances maintained for convenience with other banks. Although when these items are cleared they will increase the bank's balance at the Bank of England they cannot be regarded as a liquid asset. This is because other banks will have cheques drawn on the bank that are in the course of collection and which will reduce the balance at the Bank of England. If all the banks were to close their doors for three days and clear all the cheques and withdraw balances this item would disappear from the banks' balance sheets.

9. Certificates of deposit. A certificate of deposit is a document issued by a bank certifying that a deposit has been made with that bank which is repayable to bearer upon the surrender of the certificate at maturity. It stipulates the rate of interest and the date of repayment and is negotiable by simple delivery. Thus the holder may sell the certificate at any time at the market price, but which may be at a discount on the nominal value, and the bank has a deposit for a definite term of between three months and five years. Certificates of deposit are issued in mutliples of £10,000 with a minimum of £50,000 and a normal maximum of £500,000.

When sterling certificates of deposit were first issued in 1958 it was thought that they would attract funds from outside the banking system, but they have become more of a means of interbank borrowing and lending.

As this is an asset item in the balance sheet, it represents certificates of deposit which were issued by other banks and invested in by the bank in our example.

For certificates approaching maturity the rate of interest tends to be about the banks' base rate and it rises to about 2 per cent above base rate for certificates with a year to maturity.

10. Special Deposits. These are a weapon of the central bank and have been defined in VI, 21. They cannot be regarded as a very liquid item as they are repayable only when the authorities choose to do so. However, if the banks ran into serious liquidity problems it is inconceivable that the Bank of England would not help them out of their troubles by repaying some or all of the Special Deposits.

The level of Special Deposits has varied from time to time since they were first brought into use in 1960; at one stage they were reduced to nil and at the other extreme reached 5 per cent of sterling deposits. As there is no existing call for Special Deposits (as at the time of writing) this asset does not appear in Fig. 2.

The rate of interest on Special Deposits, when they are called for, is approximately equal to Treasury bill rate and is adjusted if necessary after each weekly tender to the nearest $\frac{1}{16}$ per cent to Treasury bill rate.

11. Investments. These are all in government stocks with varying dates to maturity. The bank will have so acquired them as to ensure that it has a fairly regular flow of maturities each year. The yield on them will depend upon the price that was paid for them and the rate of interest that is paid on their nominal value, but it is likely to be well above the banks' base rate. In addition the bank, being an institutional investor which can afford to hold stocks for a long period, may make a capital gain by buying stock at less than the nominal value and redeeming it at the nominal value on maturity.

12. Advances. The term "advances" is used to mean both loans and overdrafts. Technically all advances (other than term loans such as personal instalment loans) are repayable on demand, but in reality not a very high proportion could be repaid immediately and advances must be regarded as an illiquid asset. The rates of interest charged range from 1 per cent above base rate for the most highly favoured industrial firm to 3 per cent or more above base rate for the small private borrower. On personal instalment loans, although the nominal rate of interest may be less than base rate, the "true" rate of interest may be well above it because the interest is charged on the whole debt for the whole of the borrowing period even though it is repaid in instalments during the period.

The proportions of advances to deposits has gradually increased since 1945, but now that it stands at just over 70 per cent it is unlikely that the banks will want to increase this proportion still further. This does not mean that the total of advances will not increase — it can do so as deposits increase — but the ratio to deposits is unlikely to rise. This is because the banks must maintain a balance between lending to the private sector and the public sector of the community. In the event of a serious recession, many of the advances to firms and individuals in the private sector may become bad debts, whereas the Government sector is a much better risk! Apart from its holdings of commercial bills, leasing of plant and equipment, and investments in subsidiary companies and in premises, all assets other than advances represent lending either directly or indirectly to the Government.

13. Trade investments. These are investments in both Stock Exchange listed and unlisted companies. As a proportion of total assets this item is very small, the majority of investments by a bank being gilt-edged and appearing in the balance sheet under the heading of Investments (*see* **11** *above*).

14. Investments in associated companies. These are investments in companies in which the bank has less than 50 per cent of the shares, which means that the companies are not subsidiary companies. Examples are the Agricultural Mortgage Corporation and the Bankers' Clearing House in which all of the four main clearing banks have an interest.

Quite apart from these investments in associated companies, the banks have subsidiary companies concerned with such activities as hire-purchase, factoring, leasing and insurance, but as this is a group balance sheet these assets are incorporated into the figure for the group as a whole and not shown as a separate item in the balance sheet.

15. Premises. In view of the fact that the bank in Fig. 2 may have as many as three or four thousand branches, the total of £500 million for premises is a modest valuation.

RESERVE REQUIREMENTS AND OTHER CONTROLS

16. Central Bank controls. Quite apart from the bank's own desire to keep adequate reserves in order to be able to satisfy all its depositors' requests for repayment, a certain mixture of assets to deposits is preferred by the Bank of England, to ensure that prudence prevails.

Up to 1981 the Bank prescribed a 12½ per cent reserve requirement (reserve assets as a percentage of eligible liabilities) but no such reserve requirement is now in force. However, by virtue of the Banking Act 1979 the Bank of England keeps a close eye on the assets structure of each individual bank and will give "advice" where necessary to ensure that a bank or licensed deposit-taker improves its holding of liquid assets. Although the reserve ratio no longer applies, it would be as well if we examine what is involved.

17. Eligible liabilities. Whereas prior to September 1971, the banks maintained cash and liquidity ratios that were calculated as a proportion of their total deposits, the new arrangements prescribed quite precisely which deposits and which assets were to be used in calculating the banks' reserve ratio. The ratio was to be determined by expressing the total of reserve assets as a proportion of eligible liabilities.

Eligible liabilities comprise sterling deposit liabilities, excluding deposits having an original maturity of over two years, plus any sterling resources obtained by switching foreign currencies into sterling. Inter-bank transactions and sterling certificates of deposit (both held and issued) are taken into the calculation of individual banks' liabilities on a net basis, irrespective of term. Adjustments are also made in respect of balances with, and loans to, other monetary sector institutions, and advances to money lent to money brokers and gilt-edged jobbers.

18. Reserve assets. These comprised balances with the Bank of England (other than Special Deposits), British government and Northern Ireland government Treasury bills, company tax reserve certificates, money at call with the London money market, government stocks and stocks of nationalised industries guaranteed by the Government with one year or less to final maturity, local authority bills eligible for rediscount at the Bank of England and (up to a maximum of 2 per cent of eligible liabilities) commercial bills eligible for rediscount at the Bank of England.

19. The ratio. Prior to September 1971, only the London and Scottish clearing banks had an agreement with the Bank of England to maintain set proportions of their deposits in cash and other liquid assets, and were subjected to calls for Special Deposits. Since 1971, all banks have been brought within the Bank of England's control, thus giving the Bank of England a much more effective means of influencing bank lending as a whole, and the clearing banks have benefited by fairer competition. As part of the 1971 arrangements, the clearing banks agreed to abandon their collective agreements on interest rates.

From 1971 to 1981 the banks observed a uniform ratio of 12½ per cent of reserve assets to eligible liabilities.

The London discount houses are not obliged to make Special Deposits with the Bank of England, nor did the 12½ per cent ratio apply to them. However, by virtue of the Banking Act 1979 they are now recognised banks and as such must heed the advice of the Bank of England concerning the structure of their assets.

20. Returns to the Bank of England. The banks are required to submit regular monthly and quarterly returns to the Bank of England concerning the composition of their assets and liabilities, and the Banking Act 1979 widened the scope of these returns to include not only all recognised banks but the licensed deposit-takers as well.

The London Clearing Banks publish a statement of their assets and liabilities once a month, as at the third Wednesday in the month, and this is commented on in the *Financial Times* and other newspapers.

21. Banking Act 1979. The Banking Act 1979 had two main provisions: the licensing of deposit-takers and the establishment of the Deposit Protection Fund. The first of these provisions gave the Bank of England the power to grant or to refuse to grant applications for recognition as a bank and laid down specified criteria about which the Bank must be satisfied before granting recognition. The purpose of this control is of course to protect depositors from the unscrupulous activities of persons who might otherwise set themselves up as banks and misuse their depositors' funds. The Act distinguished between Recognised Banks and Licensed Deposit-Takers. To aspire to be a Recognised Bank an institution must satisfy much stricter criteria than it would to be a licensed deposit-taker, but the Bank imposes a much stricter degree of supervision on the lower category.

The Deposit Protection Fund protects deposits up to £10,000 for any depositor and will pay depositors three-quarters of deposits up to that sum where a deposit-taking institution becomes insolvent. The protection fund amounts to about £6 million and was raised by a levy on recognised banks and licensed institutions.

PROGRESS TEST 13

1. Why must a bank weigh the balance between profitability and liquidity? **(1)**

2. Describe the two principal liabilities on a bank balance sheet **(2)**

3. Write out a simplified balance sheet of a banking group. (*See* Fig. 2)

4. What constitutes the item "cash" in a bank balance sheet? **(3)**

5. Define call money. **(4)**

6. What are the two gentlemen's agreements in which the discount houses are concerned? **(5)**

7. How is the rate of interest on a Treasury Bill determined? **(5)**

8. What are "other bills" on a bank balance sheet and what yield do the banks expect from them? **(6)**

9. Why should the banks disregard cheques in course of collection when totalling their liquid assets? **(8)**

10. Describe a certificate of deposit. **(9)**

11. Should Special Deposits be regarded as a liquid item on a bank balance sheet? **(10)**

12. Describe the item "investments". **(11)**

13. What types of loans are included under the heading "advances"? **(12)**

14. Why would the banks be reluctant to let the ratio of advances to deposits increase much above its present level? **(12)**

15. What types of subsidary companies have the banks acquired in recent years? **(14)**

16. Explain the term "eligible liabilities". **(17)**

17. What were a bank's reserve assets within the provisions of *Competition and Credit Control*? **(18)**

18. Why do the banks have to submit detailed returns to the Bank of England? **(20)**

19. Explain how recent legislation has been devised to give protection to bank depositors. **(21)**

PART SIX

THE PRINCIPLES OF BANK LENDING

CHAPTER XIV

Types of Bank Advances

SHORT- AND MEDIUM-TERM LENDING

1. Self-liquidating advances. The British banks have in the past been rather conservative in their approach to lending, preferring short-term self-liquidating loans rather than medium- or long-term ones. Furthermore, unlike some of the banks on the Continent, they have not wished to become involved in the running of their customer's businesses. They do not, as a general rule, invest in the equity capital of a company customer nor would they expect to appoint a nominee as a director of a company to look after the bank's involvement in the firm's finances, although if a firm was in danger of having to go into liquidation the bank might appoint a person, possibly an accountant, to intervene in the company's business affairs in an endeavour to save the bank from incurring a bad debt.

As we shall see, the banks have become much more involved in medium- and long-term lending in the 1960s and 1970s, but nevertheless the principle of self-liquidation still applies to a large proportion of their advances and needs now to be considered.

An advance is said to be self-liquidating when it is to be repaid from the sale of the goods that the money will help to produce or from the maturity or redemption of the security. A few examples will help to demonstrate what is meant by the term.

A shopkeeper who is stocking up for Christmas will possibly borrow from his bank in order to do so. When the goods are sold, he repays the advance.

A manufacturer who has a new contract may borrow in order to buy materials and pay for the labour required to produce the goods. When the buyer pays for the order the manufacturer is able to pay off the loan.

Farmers borrow from seedtime to harvest, though if they have a bad harvest they may not always be able to repay what they have borrowed. It is a fact that many bank advances to farmers must be regarded as long-term even though they may have been originally taken on a short-term basis.

Another type of self-liquidating advance would be one against an insurance policy which will be repaid out of the proceeds of the policy.

2. Loans and overdrafts. Bank advances are normally provided by way of a straightforward loan or overdraft. A loan account is separate from the customer's current account and it is debited with the amount of the loan while the current account is credited. As and when repayments are made, the loan account is credited and the current account is debited. An overdraft occurs when a customer draws cheques in excess of the credit balance on his current account. This used to be called "going into the red" because overdrafts under the manual system of book-keeping were shown in red ink in both the ledger and the customer's statement. Computers and accounting machines indicate both credit balances and overdrafts in black ink with a symbol CR or DR against the balance.

3. Term loans. Until 1971 all the banks' deposits were repayable either on demand (current accounts) or within seven days (deposit accounts) and hence it was considered unwise to invest or lend more than a small part of these deposits on a long-term basis. The attitude of the banks towards longer-term lending has changed a great deal since then with the introduction of certificates of deposit, some of which have a tenor of as much as five years, with the ability to switch Eurocurrency loans into sterling, with the ability to "buy" wholesale deposits in the inter-bank market and from other sources, and with the use of subsidiary companies, especially foreign banks, to obtain longer-term deposits. Also banks now invite fixed deposits for sums of £10,000 or more for fixed periods ranging from one week to a maximum of five years at a rate of interest which is fixed at the outset. Companies must still look to their shareholders for permanent capital and to debentures for much of their really long-term finance; but medium-term finance, for the purchase of plant and equipment for instance, can now be more easily obtained from a bank or one of its subsidiary companies. In their evidence to the Committee to Review the Functioning of Financial Institutions (the Wilson

Committee) in 1977, the London Clearing Banks were able to show that contractual term loans then accounted for 40 per cent of their advances to UK residents other than the personal category, and if loans under the export finance schemes are included this proportion is increased to 47 per cent.

Term loans are normally for five to seven years, sometimes ten, and the terms are laid down in a contract. This specifies the period of the loan, the rate of interest and the timing of repayments. If the customer breaks the contract the loan is repayable immediately. Repayments are not necessarily evenly spread over the term of the loan but arranged to suit the needs of the borrower.

Through what is known as *asset and liability management* a bank is now able to adopt a very different attitude towards increasing its advances. If it makes a policy decision to increase the size of this asset (or any other asset for that matter) it can obtain additional deposits in the wholesale market and does not have to wait until it has collected sufficient additional retail deposits through its branches.

4. Personal loans. The commercial banks also provide personal instalment loans for the private borrower. These loans are available for sums of up to £5,000 or more repayable in equal monthly instalments of principal and interest over a period of two or three years. These are usually unsecured and the interest is charged on the whole loan for the whole of the period. Some secured loans for up to eight years and for up to £10,000 have also been made.

Some banks provide revolving credit loans which permit the personal customer to draw up to an agreed amount whenever he wishes. This involves the payment of a fixed amount to the bank each month and when the amount is in credit the bank pays interest on the balance.

Credit cards, e.g. Barclaycard and Access, also provide the customer with a means of obtaining credit if he requires it. Access is owned jointly by Lloyds, Midland and National Westminster banks, and Barclaycard is of course owned by Barclays. The credit card enables the holder to buy goods without payment of cash at those shops that will accept the card. At the end of each month the card holder receives a bill for the amounts spent during the month and he can either pay this in full or, alternatively, pay a part of the debt. A minimum amount which must be paid at once is usually specified on the monthly statement. Interest is paid on the outstanding debt. American Express cards and Diners cards are also credit cards, but without the facility for extended credit, as payment of the outstanding amount is normally expected shortly after the monthly account is rendered.

5. Finance for Industry. Through two institutions set up in 1945, Industrial and Commercial Finance Corporation and Finance Corporation for Industry (recently brought together under a holding company called Finance for Industry), the commercial banks and the Bank of England have been stimulating the flow of medium- and long-term capital to industry. They are majority shareholders of these institutions and with their capital plus loans and debentures which the institutions have been able to float they have been able to provide the extra finance for industry. A wide range of other financial institutions have pledged themselves to take up periodic issues of marketable stock of FFI. The corporations also invite deposits from the public and regularly advertise in the national press. They invite deposits for up to ten years and offer a rate of interest which is fixed for the term of the deposit.

6. Loans for shipbuilding and farming. The banks have jointly provided a very large sum of money by way of loans for shipbuilding under a special Government scheme and have also, as majority shareholders, provided medium- and long-term finance for farmers through the Agricultural Mortgage Corporation.

POST-SHIPMENT FINANCE

7. Loans for exports of consumer goods. Since the Second World War, the banks have provided a very substantial amount of finance to exporters on the strength of the comprehensive policies of the Export Credits Guarantee Department (ECGD). This Department, which is responsible to the Secretary of State for Trade and Industry, offers insurance to exporters against non-payment for their goods. For a small premium the Department will recompense the exporter the major part of the value of the goods if the importer cannot or will not pay. The comprehensive policies, which cover consumer goods and light engineering goods that are sold on short-term credit of up to six months, can be assigned to a bank. As they provide a excellent form of security to the banks they have been encouraged to lend on a much larger scale than they would otherwise have done. To provide even better security for the banks the comprehensive guarantee has been supplemented in recent years by guarantees by ECGD direct to the banks in return for which the banks have lent the exporter up to 100 per cent of the value of the goods in a large number of cases and at a very favourable rate of interest.

8. Finance for overseas capital projects. The ECGD has also provided policies to protect firms engaged in supplying capital goods and constructing capital projects overseas, and these policies have also brought forth bank finance which otherwise would not have been lent. Most of these capital exports are paid for over a period of five years or more, which is beyond the period of short-term lending which the banks normally expect to provide. The policies are direct between the Department and the banks and cover 100 per cent of the loan so that the banks have had a first-class form of security, as well as the bills of exchange and promissory notes which are normally used as a means of payment for capital projects. In return, the banks charge a fixed rate of interest for such loans which at times has been very low in comparison with the general level of interest rates. The Government makes up the difference between market rates of interest and those charged by the banks.

NOTE: The student need not examine the services of the Export Credits Guarantee Department in any detail at this stage but will need to do so in studying Finance of International Trade in Stage II of the Banking Diploma examinations.

BANK ADVANCES BY SECTORS

9. Quarterly returns to the Bank of England. All banks in the United Kingdom submit information to the Bank of England in February, May, August and November, analysing their advances by sectors of the community. A summary of the figures for banks in Great Britain for August 1983 is given in Table V, from which it will be seen that advances to manufacturing industry constitute approximately a fifth of total advances and personal borrowers also account for a large proportion. Other large borrowing sectors are Financial (including hire purchase and property companies), Construction, Professional, and Distribution.

COST OF BANK LOANS

10. Interest rates. Rates of interest on bank loans and overdrafts are quoted to customers in three different ways:

(a) at a margin over base rate;
(b) at a margin over LIBOR (London inter-bank offered rate);
(c) at a fixed rate.

The most common of these quotations is the first one, and for "blue chip" borrowers (large companies of national repute) the rate would

TABLE V. ADVANCES BY BANKS IN GREAT BRITAIN, August 1983

MANUFACTURING:	£ million
Food, drink and tobacco	2,650
Chemicals and allied industries	2,548
Metal manufacture	1,001
Electrical engineering	1,567
Other engineering and metal goods	3,765
Shipbuilding	899
Vehicles	981
Textiles, leather and clothing	1,169
Other manufacturing	4,638
Total	19,219
AGRICULTURE, FORESTRY AND FISHING	5,034
MINING AND QUARRYING	2,436
CONSTRUCTION	3,791
HIRE PURCHASE FINANCE HOUSES	1,563
PROPERTY COMPANIES	4,062
OTHER FINANCIAL	14,731
TRANSPORT AND COMMUNICATION	3,689
PUBLIC UTILITIES AND NATIONAL GOVERNMENT	706
LOCAL GOVERNMENT	1,462
RETAIL DISTRIBUTION	4,339
OTHER DISTRIBUTION	6,786
PROFESSIONAL, SCIENTIFIC AND MISCELLANEOUS	14,154
PERSONAL:	
House Purchase	12,154
Other	13,414
Total Advances to UK Residents	107,539
Total Advances in Sterling	84,325
Total Advances in Foreign currency	23,214
	107,539

Source: Bank of England Quarterly Bulletin

probably be 1 per cent above base rate. The larger and more influential borrower is usually able to borrow from a bank at a more favourable rate than a smaller borrower, especially the private individual who may have to pay between 3 per cent and 5 per cent above base rate. To some extent this preferential treatment is based on the fact that the smaller loans are more costly to administer as well as indicating the additional risk. Even the small firm can secure a very favourable rate of interest if it is exporting and borrows against the security of an Export Credits Guarantee Department Bills Guarantee or Open Account Guarantee when the rate charged is ⅝ per cent above base rate. The banks agreed to make this concession in return for the 100 per cent security which these ECGD guarantees give them.

LIBOR tends to be used as the basis for quotations for term loans with a margin of about 1 per cent or less for medium-term loans to "blue chip" customers and wider margins for smaller companies. Although the rate of interest is linked in this way, it tends to be adjusted only when the term loan comes up for renewal.

Fixed rates of interest apply to personal instalment loans, to fixed-interest term loans and to a medium- and long-term export and shipbuilding loans backed by ECGD. They are also used by the instalment finance subsidiaries of the banks when lending to industry and commerce.

On overdrafts the customer pays interest on his daily balance and benefits from payments into the account day by day. On a loan account, other than an instalment loan, interest is charged on the outstanding balance, but the balance changes only when repayments are made. Daily swings in the balance on the customer's current account do not affect the interest on the loan account which is quite separate. On personal instalment loans and fixed-interest term loans the interest is calculated at the outset on the sum borrowed for the whole period of the loan even though it is gradually repaid. This interest is added to the principal and the total sum is divided by the number of months the loan is for to arrive at the monthly instalments.

11. Charges. All current accounts, whether in debit or credit, are subject to charges. For personal accounts it is now usual for each bank to publish a tariff and if a minimum credit balance is maintained throughout the period (usually three or six months) no charge is made. If the balance falls below this level the charge is based on the number of debit (and sometimes credit) items with a rebate depending on the average balance of the account. Some banks make no charge at all provided the account is kept in credit. For business accounts it is usual for the bank to cost the work involved, i.e. number of debits, credits, cash handled, number of cheques collected, etc., and for the larger business the charge would be negotiated with the customer using the costing as a basis for the negotiations. Again, a rebate would usually be allowed for the worth of any average credit balance maintained.

PROGRESS TEST 14

1. What is meant by the concept of self-liquidating advances? **(1)**
2. Distinguish between a loan and an overdraft. **(2)**
3. Why is it that the banks have become more involved in medium-term lending in recent years? **(3)**
4. Explain what is meant by a term loan. **(3)**
5. What is meant by asset and liability management? **(3)**
6. What is a revolving credit loan? **(4)**
7. What are credit cards and to what extent can they be used to obtain extended credit? **(4)**
8. Distinguish between a personal instalment loan and an ordinary bank loan. **(4)**
9. Explain how the banks have stimulated a flow of medium- and long-term finance for industry through the establishment of FCI, ICFC and FFI. **(5)**
10. In what way have the services of the Export Credits Guarantee Department encouraged the banks to increase their lending for the export of consumer goods? **(7)**
11. What protection can be given to a bank when it lends money to finance an overseas capital project? **(8)**
12. Are the banks involved to any great extent in providing loans in foreign currencies? **(9)**
13. Which are the main sectors of the community that borrow from the banks? **(9)**
14. What are the three ways in which interest rates on loans and overdrafts are quoted to bank customers? **(10)**
15. Explain the basis on which some bank customers are charged higher rates of interest than others when they borrow by way of loan or overdrafts. **(10)**
16. How is the interest on a personal instalment loan calculated? **(10)**
17. Explain the basis on which bank charges are calculated in respect of (*a*) personal accounts and (*b*) business accounts. **(11)**

CHAPTER XV

Bank Lending: I

THE CRITERIA FOR LENDING

1. Basic considerations. Before a bank manager agrees to make an advance or recommends to his regional office that such an advance should be made, he must be satisfied on a number of counts. It is easy to lend money but not always easy to get it back from the borrower and while the bank must be prepared to take some risks when lending money, it does not want to incur bad debts. The questions that have to be answered are as follows:

(*a*) How much is required?
(*b*) How long is it required for?
(*c*) What is the purpose of the advance?
(*d*) Has the customer the ability to service the debt?
(*e*) What is the course of repayment?
(*f*) Is the customer creditworthy?
(*g*) How much is the customer putting into it?
(*h*) Are there any national interest considerations?
(*i*) What security is being offered?

All of these factors need to be looked at more closely and some of them in greater detail than others before the manager can make his decision as to whether to advance the money or not. They are dealt with in turn in the following sections.

2. How much and for how long. These are obvious pieces of information that must be ascertained at the outset. The customer may not know just how much he does need and may be relying on the manager to help him determine his needs. Some judicious enquires about the timing of his proposed expenditure and of his expected items of income will usually produce the required answer. A larger business concern will be continually examining its cash flow situation and should be able to furnish soundly-based information to justify the advance it requires.

These enquires should also help in deciding for how long the advance is required. This is an important consideration because the bank will not want to lend the money for an indefinite period. It will want to see the debt either gradually repaid over a fixed period or (if circumstances warrant it) repaid at the end of that agreed period. Generally the principles of short-term lending outlined in XIV still apply, though as is stated in that chapter, the banks have become much more involved in longer-term lending in recent years.

3. What is the purpose of the advance? The reason for the advance will usually determine the type of lending. If the customer is a private customer and requires finance to tide him over until his salary or some other expected payment is received an overdraft would suit his needs better than a loan or personal instalment loan. If, on the other hand, he is buying a car or large item of domestic equipment or furniture, an instalment loan would be appropriate. Similarly a business concern is likely to need an overdraft to supplement its working capital whereas a fixed loan or an instalment loan would be more appropriate for the purchase of capital equipment.

The bank must carefully consider whether the proposed purchase, e.g. of equipment or raw materials, is most suited to the needs of the firm. What are the prospects of using these purchases to advantage? Is there sufficient demand for the firm's finished product to justify the expenditure? If the customer is taking undue risks in buying the goods in that their resale is highly speculative the bank will obviously be less willing to make the advance.

4. Servicing the debt. Clearly the customer must be able to service the debt, i.e. pay the interest and charges when they are due, and for this purpose the bank will require details of his income and expenditure or that of the firm if a private customer is not involved. A customer who is living beyond his means and cannot afford to meet this commitment to the bank is hardly likely to persuade the bank to lend him the money.

5. Source of repayment. It is vital that the source of repayment is established at the outset. If it is to come from a definite source, such as the maturity of an insurance policy, sale of property, completion of a contract, or some other expected payment, then the situation is quite clear. The bank might even ensure that the repayment comes from the source by requiring the customer to sign an instruction to the insurance company or solicitor etc. concerned, to the effect that the proceeds should be paid to the bank, but we will consider this aspect more fully when we examine the techniques of taking securities. If repayment is to come from normal income then the bank is going to need to be satisfied that there will be sufficient surplus of income over expenditure for this to be possible. In the case of a firm or company the bank will want to see its cash flow forecasts to ensure that the repayments will be possible without the firm running into liquidity problems through the uneven flow of income.

6. Creditworthiness. If the customer is an established one who has had an account with the bank for some years, the manager will have the history of the account as a record of the customer's credit-worthiness. He will know, or be able to ascertain, whether the customer has run his account in a satisfactory manner. Have cheques been returned unpaid through lack of funds? Has the customer overdrawn his account without making prior arrangements? Has he repaid previous advances in the way and in the time he said he would? Has he maintained a reasonable average balance over the years? If the customer is a relatively new one (or possibly a brand new one seeking a personal instalment loan) then enquiries must be made through his previous bank, if there was one, or through a credit-reporting agency.

The bank manager may know his customer and his business quite well and be able to assess his business acumen and his credit-worthiness from that knowledge. If the firm is a large one then it will have a local, and possibly a national, reputation on which to make a judgment. A number of previous years' balance sheets would be helpful in assessing creditworthiness, as we see later in this chapter.

7. The customer's own contribution. A reasonable basis on which to work is that the customer must be expected to put some of his own money into the asset he is buying or venture in which he is going to become involved. He cannot expect the bank to take all the risk. If he has sufficient confidence in the future success of the venture then he must demonstrate it by putting in some of the capital required. The extent to which he might be expected to do this must of course depend upon the particular purpose of the loan and the extent to which the bank is already committed. For instance, if a retailer wants to stock up for the increased sales at Christmas and his own capital is already locked up in the business and he owes very little to the bank or to any other creditor, then the bank might well be prepared to lend him all that is required for the new stock. Whereas someone setting up a new shop might be required to find a high percentage of the capital needed from his own resources. A good rule of thumb is that the firm should be expected to have at least an equal share in the venture to that of the bank and other lenders. The proprietor's own resources should be sufficient to meet the normal trading risks plus a little more besides. The term "gearing" is used to describe the ratio between the proprietor's own resources and the total borrowing of the business, and where the proprietor's share is less than 50 per cent the gearing ratio is said to be high.

8. National interest considerations. The banks have been given Government guidance from time to time as to which sectors of the community should be given priority when it comes to making advances (qualitative directives). For instance, that the banks should give priority to exporters, to defence industries and to farmers. On the other hand the banks have been advised that they should not lend for speculative reasons. These considerations must be borne in mind by a bank in deciding whether or not to make a particular advance and it is conceivable that the Government's request to give special consideration to exporters would weigh the balance in an exporter's favour when his application for an advance was not otherwise acceptable.

9. What security is being offered? By no means are all advances secured, i.e. backed by the lodgment of some form of security such as deeds of property or stocks and shares; indeed a large proportion of them are made purely on the creditworthiness of the borrower. The purpose of lodging some form of security is of course to provide the bank with an asset which can be relied upon to produce the funds with which to repay the advance should the customer fail to do so, but the last thing the bank wants to do is to realise the funds in this way. The bank will want to ensure either that it has a legal title to the asset or that written instructions are given for the proceeds of its sale or redemption to be sent to the bank. The various ways in which securities can be taken by a bank and the various types of securities need now to be considered in some detail.

TAKING SECURITIES

10. Lien. A lien gives a banker rather special right to retain property belonging to a borrower until he has repaid the advance. In that the banker has the right, the owner of the property cannot get it back to make alternative use of it except by extinguishing the debt. The bank, on the other hand, has no right to sell the property as the title to it remains with the customer.

A banker's lien does not apply to securities that are deposited only for safe custody because they have been deposited by the customer for that particular purpose. However it does apply to all documents that come into the banker's possession in the ordinary course of his business, including cheques and bills of exchange paid in for collection. The lien applies only if the customer has a loan or overdraft, not if he is in credit, and once the banker parts with the security concerned he loses his right to claim a lien on it.

11. Pledge. When goods or documents of title to goods are pledged to a bank, the bank has a right to retain them until the debt is repaid, and can sell the goods if the debt is not repaid. The bank (the pledgee) must pay over to the pledgor any surplus remaining after liquidating the debt and may sell without recourse to a court. The types of securities subject to pledge are goods and chattels and negotiable securities, such as bearer bonds.

12. Mortgage. The interest in such securities as title deeds to property, life policies and stocks and shares may be conveyed to a bank by way of mortgage which may be a legal or an equitable mortgage. A legal mortgage conveys the ownership of the property to the mortgagee (the person to whom the property is mortgaged, e.g. the bank) who has the right to do what he wishes with the property. On the other hand, an equitable mortgage conveys only a claim to the property and the bank may have to compete with others who hold similar claims to it. Clearly a legal mortgage is much more secure from the banker's point of view than an equitable mortgage.

13. Assignment. Debts due or accruing due to a person may be assigned to another person. Therefore money due to a customer under a contract, the sale of property such as a life policy, or under a will, may be assigned to the bank. An assignment must be unconditional and must be in writing. Notice of it must be given in writing to the debtor concerned, i.e. to the person who owes the money to the bank's customer.

14. Stocks and shares. Although the terms "stocks" and "shares" are frequently used as if they are one and the same thing there is a clear distinction between them. A "stock" represents a debt owed by central or local government or from some institution or company which is registered in a person's name. He is paid interest on the stock, usually at a rate agreed when it is issued, e.g. 7 per cent Treasury Stock, 9 per cent Debenture Stock, and it may be redeemable at a fixed date, between two given dates (e.g. 7 per cent Treasury Stock 1989–91), or at some indefinite time (e.g. 3 per cent War Loan). The term "share" means a part-ownership and the person in whose name it is registered is one of the proprietors of the company concerned. If a company's issued capital is divided up into 100,000 shares each share represents the ownership of one hundred-thousandth part of the firm.

The ownership of stocks and shares is registered in the name of the person who has bought them, and he is issued with a certificate indicating this fact. He can transfer the ownership to another person by completing a stock transfer form and sending it with the certificate to the registrar of the company or of the Government or other official body concerned. When the transfer has been registered a new certificate is issued in the name of the new owner.

When taking stocks and shares as security the banker will take a memorandum of deposit. This is a legal document in which the customer declares his intention to charge the security and authorises the bank to acquire legal ownership if it wishes to do so. The customer undertakes to complete whatever forms the bank requires to complete its security.

15. Bearer bonds. Unlike stocks and shares, bearer bonds are negotiable instruments, the ownership of which passes from hand to hand by delivery. The bonds are issued in respect of money lent to a company or institution and interest is paid on them at stipulated periods. As the names of the owners of the bonds are not registered the interest has to be claimed by producing the appropriate coupon attached to the bond. Sheets of coupons are attached comprising one for each interest payment and these have to be cut off as they fall due.

When a bank makes an advance against the security of bearer bonds it can complete its security quite simply by having the bonds delivered to it if they are not already in its possession, and taking a memorandum of deposit. This latter is necessary as proof that the bonds are lodged as security and not for safe custody. The bank is then able to sell them, if necessary, whereas it is not able to transfer securities on safe custody.

16. Advances against title deeds. An owner of land (which includes the buildings on it as well as mines etc.) has his title to it registered in the form of a title deed called a Land Registry Certificate. Virtually all land is now registered land, i.e. the name of the owner is recorded by the Land Registry, but some still remains unregistered with the claim to ownership resting in the possession of a bundle of deeds. These deeds must show a chain of title over a period of at least fifteen years and if the land is sold the solicitor acting for the owner has to prove this title. This proof of title has become much simpler with the conversion to registered land in that the registered land certificate is proof of title and it is only necessary to send it to the Land Registry to have it brought up to date.

The title to land may be freehold or leasehold. If it is freehold the title is as absolute as possible but if it is leasehold it expires over a given period of years and reverts back to the freeholder who has granted the leasehold for that period. Ground rent is payable by the leaseholder to the freeholder and if this is not paid the freeholder can bring the leasehold to an end. A bank taking title deeds as security must therefore check whether the title is freehold or leasehold and, if the latter, must check when the leasehold expires and that the ground rent is properly paid. There is one other category of land, *crownhold*, which is not very common and applies only to land acquired by the Land Commission and regranted by the Crown on sale or by lease.

The action to be taken by a banker to perfect the bank's security must depend upon whether he wants an equitable mortgage or a legal mortgage on the land and upon whether it is registered or unregistered. If only an equitable mortgage is required (*see* **12** *above*) the customer will be required to sign the bank's appropriate form and in respect of non-registered land the bank will carry out searches on the Land Charges register and the Town and Country Planning registers to ensure that there are no factors that will reduce the value of the property, but will not seek to become owner of the property. The bank will continue to hold the title deeds. If there is a registered title, the bank sends the land certificate to the Land Registry with an appropriate Land Registry form to have the bank's equitable claim against the property recorded in the Register and on the land certificate, which is returned to the bank. If a legal mortgage of unregistered land is required the bank, in addition to requiring a solicitor to check the chain of title and to produce a report on title, will carry out local searches and have the title of the property transferred to it by way of the legal mortgage. For a legal mortgage of registered land the bank must check with the Land Registry that there are no prior claims on the land and, if not, send the land certificate and its own form of mortgage document to the Registry to have the mortgage registered. The two documents are kept by the Land Registry and the bank is issued with a Charge Certificate. Until the debt has been repaid and the bank notifies the Land Registry that the mortgage is to be cancelled, the Registry will not return the land certificate to the customer.

17. Life policies as secutiry. When lending against a life policy the banker takes a form of assignment from the customer, as well as the policy itself, and notifies the insurance company of the assignment. Most life policies have a surrender value, i.e. an amount which the insurance company will pay to the policy-holder on cancellation of the policy prior to its reaching maturity date, and the bank could always surrender the policy for that amount to obtain immediate repayment, or partial repayment, of the debt. The surrender value increases year by year with the payment of additional premiums. The two main types of life policies are endowment and whole life policies (*see* V, **5**).

18. Guarantees. A guarantee is satisfactory as a form of security only if the person who signs the guarantee is himself credit worthy to the extent of the debt. He is, after all, saying to the bank that if X does not repay his advance then he will in his stead. The guarantor may be required to deposit some form of security himself as backing for his guarantee.

LENDING TO LIMITED COMPANIES

19. Separate entities. Limited companies are separate entities and therefore call for special treatment when a loan is being considered. It is the company that is borrowing the money and not the directors or executives who may negotiate the loan.

There are two documents which must be checked by the banker before making such a loan; they are the *memorandum of association* and the *articles of association*. The *memorandum of association* indicates, among other things, the power of the company to borrow money and the purposes for which it can be borrowed. The *articles of association* indicate the extent to which the directors are permitted to commit the company without a meeting of the company.

It is possible for a company to charge its various assets such as negotiable instruments passing through its hands and documents of title to goods, but this would usually be done by taking a debenture which is something peculiar to limited companies. A debenture takes the form of an acknowledgment of a debt and may be accompanied by a fixed or floating charge over the assets of the company when it is known as a mortgage debenture. A fixed charge is a charge over the fixed assets of the company, i.e. the land which includes the building thereon. A floating charge covers the assets other than fixed assets, such as stock of raw materials and finished products and work in progress. The usual type of debenture taken by a bank gives a charge on all assets of the company both fixed and floating and usually the bank also requires a legal mortgage over the real property of the company.

OTHER TYPES OF BORROWER

20. Minors. As we saw in XI, a minor should not normally be allowed to borrow, as the bank is not able to enforce repayment in that any contract is void under the Infants' Relief Act 1874. The banks do lend to minors on occasions, however, quite often on the basis of a verbal understanding with a parent. Should security for an advance be necessary it is possible for a bank to take an indemnity from someone other than the minor—a guarantee must not be taken because a minor cannot be a principal debtor. An indemnity makes the person giving the indemnity directly liable for the debt instead of indirectly liable as he would be under a guarantee.

21. Executors. As we saw in XI, personal representatives whether executors or administrators often need to borrow in order to settle the capital transfer tax on the deceased's estate. If capital transfer tax is payable then the estate must be a substantial one and there should be assets which can be used to support the advance. The bank will enter into an understanding with the executors as to which of the assets are to be sold to repay the advance and will require them to sign a form of charge which makes them personally liable for the borrowing.

Borrowing may also be permitted (unless the will states otherwise) to enable the personal representatives to pay off the deceased's debts pending the disposal of assets, and again they must be made jointly and personally liable for the borrowing although they are entitled to be indemnified out of the estate.

22. House buyers. The banks provide bridging loans to customers who are selling one house and buying another to cover the gap between receiving the proceeds from the sale and having to pay for the purchase. The bridging loan is usually necessary to pay the 10 per cent deposit on the new property which has to be paid on signing the contract, but if the sale and purchase are not synchronised it will be needed to pay for the whole of the purchase pending receipt of the proceeds.

The bank will work in conjunction with the solicitor the customer has engaged to carry out the sale and purchase, and will require an undertaking from that solicitor to pay over the proceeds of the sale to the bank and to send the deeds of the new property to the bank on completion of the purchase. This will be particularly necessary if the bank is providing mortgage finance for the property being purchased where, of course, the deeds are the bank's security. The bank will have to ensure that its own form of mortgage is completed by the customer.

23. Business loans. When a bank is lending to a business (other than to a limited company which we have dealt with above) it will need to make sure that the proprietors are made fully liable for the debt. In the case of a sole trader, the customer is fully liable for the business and the advance will be in his name. The security, if any, will be deposited in the proprietor's own name. If the customer has produced sets of accounts the bank may wish to see them.

When lending to a partnership the bank will, through its mandate signed by the partners when they opened the account, have established that the partners are jointly and severally liable for the debt. When the advance is negotiated all the partners should agree in writing.

THE CONSUMER CREDIT ACT 1974

24. Lending to consumers. Under the Consumer Credit Act 1974 all institutions which are concerned with consumer credit services, including banks, finance houses, credit rating organisations, and debt-collecting agencies and brokers arranging credit terms for customers, have to be licensed by the Director General of Fair Trading. The Act covers a wide range of businesses such as car dealers and double-glazing contractors and licences, which have to be renewed every three years, can be withdrawn if the licensee does not comply with the terms of the licence.

All borrowers other than limited companies are protected by the Act, up to a maximum borrowing of £5,000. It does not apply to ordinary trade credit, nor to credit in respect of foreign trade or house mortgage. All consumer purchases must indicate the cash price of the goods or the amount of the loan, the total charge for credit (TCC), the number and amount of instalments, and the total sum payable. True rates of interest as an annual percentage rate (APR) must be given for all types of transactions, so that purchasers are both aware of the real cost of buying goods by instalments and able to compare terms with those offered elsewhere. When a borrower enters into an agreement he has three days in which to change his mind. Where a borrower repays before the end of the credit period, he is entitled by the law to a rebate of some of the credit charges.

Banks are now required, as a result of the Act, to provide customers who borrow with a written agreement. Customers with overdrafts must be sent a statement shortly after interest has been debited to their accounts. It is an offence to canvass loans outside bank premises, but this means actually physically canvassing and not writing or telephoning. It does not apply to soliciting for an agreement with an existing customer to overdraw the account.

The Office of Fair Trading, which issues the licences under the Consumer Credit Act, was established by the Fair Trading Act 1973. The Director General of Fair Trading took over the functions of the Registrar of Restrictive Trading Agreements and has the added responsibility for discovering potential monopoly situations and uncompetitive practices.

PROGRESS TEST 15

1. List the factors that have to be taken into account by a bank in considering an application for an advance. **(1)**

2. Why is it important for a bank to know how long an advance is required for? **(2)**

3. Is the purpose of an advance important? **(3)**

4. What is meant by servicing a debt? **(4)**

5. Why is the source of repayment of such importance to a bank? **(5)**

6. What is meant by creditworthiness and how can it be ascertained? **(6)**

7. Why is a bank customer expected to put up some of the capital required for a project? **(7)**

8. What is meant by capital gearing? **(7)**

9. What are the possible national interest considerations in relation to bank advances? **(8)**

10. Explain what is meant by security for an advance. **(9)**

11. Define a lien. Does it apply to safe custodies? **(10)**

12. What is a pledge? What types of securities are subject to a pledge? **(11)**

13. Distinguish between a legal mortgage and an equitable mortgage. **(12)**

14. What is meant by the assignment of an asset? **(13)**

15. Distinguish between stocks and shares. **(14)**

16. What is a memorandum of deposit? **(14)**

17. Explain the significance of bearer bonds. Why do they have coupons attached to them? **(15)**

18. Distinguish between registered land and unregistered land. **(16)**

19. Distinguish between freehold and leasehold property. **(16)**

20. What is crownhold land? **(16)**

21. Explain the action that has to be taken by a banker to perfect the bank's security where there is (*a*) a legal mortgage and (*b*) an equitable mortgage on land. **(16)**

22. What action does a banker take when taking a life policy as security for an advance? **(17)**

23. What is the most important consideration when taking a guarantee as security for an advance? **(18)**

24. Which two documents need to be checked by a banker before making an advance to a limited company? **(19)**

25. Define a debenture. **(19)**

26. Distinguish between a fixed charge and a floating charge over the assets of a company. **(19)**

27. What form of security, if any, is possible when lending to a minor? **(20)**

28. What formalities are required when an advance is made to personal representatives? **(21)**

29. Describe a bridging loan and explain the formalities involved. **(22)**

30. What is involved in lending money to (*a*) sole traders and (*b*) partnerships? **(23).**

31. What are the requirements of the Consumer Credit Act as far as the banks are concerned? **(24)**

CHAPTER XVI

Bank Lending: II

LENDING AGAINST BALANCE SHEETS

1. Final accounts. The purpose of this book is not to teach the reader accounting, and it must be assumed that he or he knows sufficient about the subject to be able to understand the references to the firm's final accounts (i.e. manufacturing account, trading account, profit and loss account and balance sheet) made in this chapter. The student preparing for Stage 1 of the Institute of Bankers Banking Diploma will be studying accounting concurrently with Elements of Banking on his National Certificate, National Diploma or a Bankers Conversion Course. The general reader who may need some help in understanding final accounts is referred to *Principles of Accounts* by E. F. Castle and N. P. Owens in the M & E HANDBOOK series.

2. Private and corporate customers. Bank customers range in type from the private individual at the one extreme to the corporate body (the limited company or institution, e.g. nationalised industry) at the other. In between are the one-man business and the partnership.

The private individual, although he might conceivably keep a close account of his income and expenditure, will not present his bank with his balance sheet and ask to borrow on the strength of it. He might well give an indication of his personal assets and offer to use one or more of them as security for an advance, but that is all.

The self-employed person would need to keep some account of his one-man business for tax purposes and may produce a balance sheet. This is useful, and all the more so if he presents a run of balance sheets over a period of three years or more. However, his balance sheets do not necessarily show all of his personal assets, such as his house, but as he is personally liable for all the transactions of his business, these personal assets can be relied upon in the event of his business running into financial difficulties. The banker then must ascertain what these assets are and use this information to supplement that to be found in the balance sheet.

A bank usually ensures that the partners in a firm are all jointly and severally liable for the debts to the bank. The firm's balance sheet therefore needs to be supplemented by a knowledge of the personal assets of the partners as does that of the one-man business.

It is for the corporate borrower, the limited company, which has its own entity quite apart from that of the proprietors, that balance sheets are especially important. They show the assets and liabilities of the company and unless they include a personal guarantee from the directors or the authorised share-capital is not fully paid up, there is no claim upon the assets of the proprietors. The size of the business is likely to be such that its affairs are much more complicated than those of the sole-proprietor or partnership so that there must be much more reliance upon the balance sheet (and indeed upon the final accounts as a whole). In the following sections of this chapter attention will therefore be paid to the factors applied to lending against balance sheets to limited companies, but these factors apply equally well to non-corporate customers. One factor that is not common to both corporate and non-corporate borrowers is of course that the borrowing powers of the company are limited by the memorandum and articles of association (*see* XV, **19**).

3. Simplified balance sheet and trading accounts. A balance sheet gives a picture of the assets and liabilities of the firm at a particular date and should be accompanied by the trading and profit and loss account for the year up to that date. The following simplified trading and profit and loss account and balance sheet will serve to illustrate the type of information the banker should look for when considering an application for an advance. In reality published accounts are much more complex and the banker must summarise them for his own purposes to simplify his task of producing the required details.

Epson
Rechargeable Batteries Ltd

Trading and Profit and Loss Account
1984

Variable cost of sales	£150,000	Sales	£250,000
Depreciation	30,000		
Administration expenses	32,500		
Net profit	37,500		
	£250,000		£250,000

Balance Sheet 31st December 1984

Share capital	£200,000	Fixed assets:		
Profit and loss account	75,000	Cost		£300,000
		less Depreciation		
	275,000			100,000
				200,000

Current liabilities:			Current assets:			
General	25,000		Stock	62,500		
Dividend	25,000	50,000	Debtors	37,500		
			Cash	25,000	125,000	
		£325,000			£325,000	

4. Reliance on creditor finance. The bank must satisfy itself that the company is not relying too much on creditors to finance its activities, and that this reliance was not increasing year by year. In our example the net worth of the company is £275,000 (the amount due to be paid to shareholders on winding up), and this is represented on the assets side by not only fixed assets (£200,000) but by £75,000 of the current assets as well. This is a healthy state of affairs for it means that the proprietors have financed the factory and equipment required to make the goods, and also much of the capital required to provide the materials, to allow stocks to be held, and credit to be granted to customers. Only £25,000 of their activities is financed from taking credit. Over the years some of the profit of the company should be ploughed back into the business and used to make fuller and more profitable use of the fixed assets, if that is possible, and additional fixed assets if they are required.

5. Working capital. The most important part of the balance sheet from a banker's point of view is that which shows the net current assets, i.e. the amount of current assets remaining after current liabilities have been deducted. By deducting the current liabilities from the current assets in this way we arrive at the working capital of the firm and this must be enough to enable the company to meet its day-to-day needs without running into liquidity problems. It must be able to buy fuel and materials, market the goods and pay wages on time. In our sample balance sheet the current assets, stock, debtors and cash amount to £125,000, while the current liabilities, creditors and the dividend due to shareholders, amount to £50,000. The working capital is therefore £75,000 of which a third is actually in cash (i.e. a credit bank balance). This is a healthy state of affairs for, although there is no hard and fast rule, a current ratio of at least 2:1 is considered desirable and our company has a ratio of 2½:1. The ratio shows the relationship of current assets (£125,000) to current liabilities (£50,000).

6. Comparative accounts. The satisfactory state of affairs indicated by a balance sheet may in fact mask a deteriorating situation over a period of years and that is why reference must be made to the balance sheets for previous years and to the trading and profit and loss accounts as well. Furthermore, the company's bank account must show plenty of activity and vigorous swings in the outstanding balance from day to day. A rather dormant account suggests a stagnant business which is having difficulty in selling its goods. Reference to the trading and profit and loss accounts will enable the banker to ascertain the turnover (total sales) and to see whether this has risen, levelled off or fallen. Also the gross profit can be calculated as a proportion of turnover and this proportion compared not only with those of previous years but also with the recognised rate of gross profit for the particular type of trade. In our example gross profit is £100,000 (sales less variable costs of sales) on a turnover of £250,000, i.e. 40 per cent. The net profit of £37,500 is a yield of 18¾ per cent on the share capital which is a higher return than could be expected from a safe investment.

Comparing the final accounts year with year will also enable the banker to ascertain a number of other facts. Have stocks and work in progress built up while turnover has not been increasing, suggesting over-production? Have creditors increased faster than debtors, i.e. has the company found it difficult to sell its goods? Have liquid assets diminished yet the output of the company not been expanded? This would suggest that overheads have risen faster than the business has increased in size.

By looking at a series of accounts the banker can thus produce much more of a moving picture of the company's activities and when making an advance do so with much more confidence than would be possible by relying on the current balance sheet alone.

7. Effect of advance on the balance sheet. When a company borrows money and uses it to acquire assets, the structure of its balance sheet will change. The banker must take this into account and, from a draft of what the balance sheet will look like, consider the consequences. For instance, if the company in our example (*see* 3 above) is lent £100,000 to buy new plant and machinery its balance sheet will become as follows:

Share capital		£200,000	Fixed assets:		
Profit and loss account		75,000	Cost		£400,000
			less Depreciation		100,000
					300,000
Current liabilities:			Current assets:		
General	25,000		Stock	62,500	
Dividend	25,000		Debtors	37,500	
					100,000
Bank					
overdraft	75,000	125,000			
		£400,000			£400,000

The credit balance with the bank (£25,000 shown as cash) has disappeared and an overdraft of £75,000 created, but it must be assumed that the overdraft will swing, possibly up to the full cost of the machinery (£100,000) because the credit balance of £25,000 was presumably being maintained for a purpose, i.e. to meet day-to-day running expenses, stock fluctuations etc. The working capital has now become a negative quantity as current assets are less than current liabilities. If the bank advance was taken by way of loan (for £100,000) rather than overdraft, thus keeping the credit balance of £25,000 for day-to-day needs, the current liabilities would amount to £150,000 and the current assets to £125,000 and still give a negative working capital.

The net worth of the company (£275,000 of capital and profit and loss) no longer covers the fixed assets, which it should do (*see* **4** *above*). Furthermore, the introduction of the new machinery is going to call for more materials, labour, and other variable costs; yet there is no working capital to provide for this expansion of output. The directors may be confident that if they can buy the additional machinery their sales and therefore profits will increase to justify its purchase, and this may well be so if there could be sufficient working capital available to meet their needs. What can the bank do under these circumstances? One solution is to suggest that, if possible, the company increases its share capital to cover the cost of the new fixed assets or that it borrows on a medium- or long-term basis. The current liabilities and current assets then remain as they were on our original balance sheet, giving a sizeable working capital which could be increased if need be by a short-term overdraft to provide the extra liquidity needed in the immediate period as output increases. The bank might of course be prepared to provide medium-term finance by way of a term loan for, say, ten years repayable in annual instalments and secured by a charge over the assets of the company. Whatever decision is made by the bank in dealing with a request for an advance it will be based not only upon the balance sheet but on the other factors so far considered and especially upon the bank's opinion of the integrity, ability and experience of the people it is dealing with.

8. Valuation of assets. The fixed assets of the company are usually valued realistically at their cost less depreciation and if the company is looked upon as a going concern, i.e. one that is to continue with little fear of it being wound up, the company's valuation of these and its current assets might be used in deciding whether or not to make an advance. However, bankers are usually more cautious than this and value the assets for their purposes on a gone concern or forced-sale basis, i.e. what they would fetch if they had to be sold immediately in order to repay the advance. It is conceivable that the buildings might be undervalued in the balance sheet, for property values may have risen steeply since the asset was purchased, in which case it would be quite safe to use the balance sheet valuation as it stands. However, if the buildings are specialised and would have to be considerably adapted by a would-be buyer the forced-sale value would be much lower.

Plant and machinery, unless it is very modern and in first-class condition, would have to be written down drastically (similarly tools, fixtures and fittings and stock in hand). Much would depend upon the particular trade and the likely demand for these items. The debtors of the business may not all pay up and therefore it would be wise to make a generous allowance for bad debts and write down the value of this asset accordingly.

9. Supervision of advances. Quite apart from the need to ensure that the security is properly charged to the bank and that, if necessary, it is adequately covered by insurance and the premium regularly paid, the bank must have a system of control whereby the progress of each advance is regularly examined. If an overdraft limit is exceeded this matter is automatically referred to the manager who must decide whether or not to pay the cheque that causes the excess, and at an agreed interval (usually a year though possibly less) each advance comes up for renewal. The customer may be invited to visit the bank to discuss the matter and a revised overdraft or loan limit is agreed for the next year (or shorter period). Normally the limit would be reduced year by year but this need not be so if, for instance, the customer can show that there has been an increase in the turnover which has necessitated more stocks and debtors and the bank is quite happy with the position. In the case of a farming advance it is by no means uncommon for a bank to find that what was meant to be a short-term advance has become long-term as a result of a run of bad harvests.

There must also be a system for revaluing the bank's security at fixed intervals. An up-to-date surrender value for an endowment insurance policy will be ascertained, stocks and shares will be revalued at market prices and property pledged to the bank will have to be viewed and its value assessed. Where an agricultural advance is concerned the bank manager will have to "walk the farm" occasionally and endeavour to put a value to the stock and crops.

PROGRESS TEST 16

1. What is meant by a firm's final accounts? **(1)**

2. When lending to a self-employed person what information will a bank require in addition to that given in his balance sheets? **(2)**

3. Is the balance sheet of a partnership sufficient in itself for a bank's purposes? **(2)**

4. Why is the balance sheet of a limited company especially important to a lending banker? **(2)**

5. Why should a bank be concerned with the extent to which a limited company is relying on finance by creditors? **(4)**

6. What is meant by working capital? **(5)**

7. Define the term "current ratio". **(5)**

8. Why does a bank require to see a series of final accounts covering a number of years? **(6)**

9. Describe the possible effects on a company's balance sheet of an advance to acquire capital equipment. Why might a bank insist that the company should obtain more capital from its shareholders instead of borrowing short-term? **(7)**

10. Distinguish between valuing assets on a going concern and gone concern basis. **(8)**

11. How are advances supervised by a bank? **(9)**

PART SEVEN

METHODS OF PAYMENT AND OTHER BANK SERVICES

CHAPTER XVII

Inland Methods of Payment

DEBIT ITEMS

1. Definition. All items that are charged to a customer's account by a bank are debit items, i.e. his account is debited. The main debits are the cheques which the customer draws, others include standing order payments and direct debits. These will be examined in detail in the following sections. Most, but not all, cheques are payable to a customer of another branch of the bank or of another bank, and hence they need to be cleared, i.e. they constitute the debit clearing. The clearing house system also will need to be examined.

2. Cheques. The definition and an illustration of a cheque are given in XII and the reader is advised to refer back to that chapter at this stage to remind himself of the functions of a cheque.

Although the use of credit transfers under the bank giro (*see* **5** *below*) has rapidly increased since they were introduced in 1960, the cheque is still by far the most commonly used method of payment apart from cash.

On each cheque the code number of the bank and branch is printed on the top right-hand corner (*see* Fig. 1). In addition there is a code line along the bottom of the cheque which is printed in special ink that is capable of being magnetised. This enables cheques to be sorted automatically and a computer is able to record details on magnetic tape. The line contains four sets of figures, the cheque number, the bank and branch number, and the customer's number. The fourth set of characters is printed either at the branch at which the cheque is paid in or at the clearing department and it is the amount of the cheque. Obviously this information will not be printed in the cheque book in advance as the amount of each cheque is not known until the drawer writes it in when drawing the cheque.

The cheque is both a safe and a convenient method of payment. It is an especially safe means of payment when it is crossed because it can be paid only through a bank account and therefore can be traced if it is stolen. Another safety aspect is that payment of a lost cheque can be countermanded. Businessmen, especially retailers, find it much safer to make and receive payments by cheque as this reduces the need to hold cash with the obvious dangers that would be entailed in storing and transferring cash. Businessmen also prefer to pay wages by cheque (or by transfer direct to the employee's bank account), and more and more workers are agreeing to this method of payment. The availability of automated teller machines is likely to increase the use of bank accounts and hence of cheques.

A cheque book is much easier to carry around than large amounts of cash. Furthermore, cheques may be sent through the post and they can be made out for any amount thus obviating the need for change. Transactions can be settled by cheque at any time and it is not necessary to wait until the banks are open to collect cash. Time is saved in counting cash and in taking it to and from the banks. Cheques are also convenient in that they may be post-dated and handed to the payee to make claims for payments as they fall due.

Another advantage of a cheque is that it is negotiable and can be passed from hand to hand provided that it is indorsed. It also serves as evidence of payment so that no receipt is necessary and a record of the transaction appears on the drawer's bank statement.

Cheques are cheap to use in comparison with some other methods of payment such as money orders and postal orders, provided of course that the drawer does not incur bank charges. Furthermore, writing a cheque does provide a modest period of credit while the cheque is being cleared quite apart from any delay by the payee in paying the cheque into his account.

3. Standing order payments. If a customer has regular payments to make, such as an insurance premium or a subscription to a club, he can authorise his bank to make the payments on his behalf. The bank will then make the payments automatically when they fall due and relieve the customer of the trouble of writing out cheques and indeed of remembering the due dates.

4. Direct debits. Organisations such as insurance companies, that receive a large number of regular payments remitted to their accounts in a variety of ways under standing-order arrangements made by their customers, can opt to use the direct debit system. This gives them a much better check on which payments have been received because it is the institution that is to receive the money that prepares the standard vouchers and then remits them for clearing through its own bank as it would cheques. A direct debit is rather similar in effect to a cheque, but instead of being an instruction signed by the bank customer (J. Smith) to pay the ABC Insurance Company, it is an instruction signed by the ABC Insurance Company to debit the account of J. Smith. Obviously the organisation concerned (the insurance company in our example) must obtain the approval of its customer to use this system and the customer's bank will want a written instruction authorising it to debit his account.

Much of the direct debiting process is now done by computer and paper vouchers are no longer necessary (*see* **10** *below*).

CREDIT ITEMS

5. Bank giro system. This system provides a means of payment for both customers and non-customers of the banks. By using a credit transfer, i.e. a bank giro credit form, a bank can be instructed to credit an account either at that branch or at another branch or bank. The person whose account is to be credited could be the person paying in the money (if he was not near his own bank) but is more likely to be a third person (or firm) who has agreed to receive payment to the credit of his account in this way. The person initiating the credit transfer pays cash and/or a cheque over the counter at a bank convenient to him, quoting on the giro slip the number of the account to be credited together with the name of the account holder and the code number of the bank and branch to which the payment is to be sent. The system saves the payee the trouble of writing a cheque and posting it, with some indication of what it is for, to the beneficiary. The latter is saved the trouble of having to take the cheque to his bank to pay it in. However, the beneficiary might prefer to receive the cheque and his invoice and thus be more readily able to check that the payment is made and to what it relates. Where a customer of a bank has several payments to make through the giro system (such as a firm paying salaries to its employees) he produces a bank giro credit slip for each payee in the normal way and in addition a summary slip giving the names and banks of the payees and the amounts. He then draws one cheque payable to his bank for the total amount.

BANK CLEARING SYSTEM

6. Debit clearing. The Bankers' Clearing House in London was established in 1833 to facilitate the daily exchange of cheques between banks and a daily settlement. The present-day ownership and administration of the London Clearing House is vested in the Committee of London Clearing Bankers, which consists of the chairmen of the clearing banks, i.e. Barclays, Coutts, Lloyds, Midland, National Westminster and Williams and Glyn's. The Trustee Savings Bank for England and Wales, the Co-operative Bank, the National Girobank and the Bank of England are also members but not shareholders. Radical changes in the structure of the payments clearing systems are about to take place which will involve the establishment of three individual clearing companies for General Clearing and Credit Clearing; CHAPS and Town Clearing; and BACS respectively. Shareholding membership of these companies will be available to financial institutions which meet prescribed criteria and, as a result, the number of clearing banks is likely to be substantially increased.

On each working day, the Bankers' Clearing House handles more than seven million cheques worth on average about £27,000 million. In the year, this amounts to over £6,800,000,000,000. These facts indicate the importance of the cheque system and indeed of the banking system in our community. Without the cheque as a method of settling day-to-day transactions our industrial and commercial development would have been much less rapid than it has been.

7. The clearing system. Branch banks sort into bank order all the cheques drawn on other banks that are paid in by their customers and send them up to their own clearing department in London. Each bundle is accompanied by a list giving the total as well as the value of each individual cheque.

A clearing bank will receive from each of its branches a bundle of cheques drawn on each of the clearing banks. Cheques for £10,000 or more on City Offices are extracted and put through the Town Clearing whereby cheques are presented by messenger for payment the same day. As far as the General Clearing is concerned, the bank's clearing department, having checked the totals of the bundles, will amalgamate them so as to produce a large "parcel" of cheques on each of the banks. Each of these large parcels will be accompanied by the listing slips for all of the bundles and a summary of them. The clearing department then delivers the parcels of cheques to the representatives of the other banks at the clearing house. These are then taken from the clearing house to the respective clearing departments of the banks where the totals are agreed with the listings. After this the cheques are sorted into branch order and the information on them is fed into the bank's computer but it is not put through (that is, the customers' accounts are not debited) until the next day. The cheques are then despatched to the branches on which they are drawn.

Settlement between the banks for the clearing takes place the day after the cheques have actually been exchanged. This is because the cheques do not reach the branches on which they are drawn until that day and they are then either paid or returned unpaid. Unpaid cheques are returned direct to the bank branch where the cheque was paid in and the clearing department is informed in order that the customer's account should not be debited.

8. Credit clearing. Since 1960 the Bankers' Clearing House has operated a credit clearing system which works in rather a similar fashion to the general clearing but the vouchers that are used represent payments due to, and not payments received from, other banks. They are the credit transfers under the Bank Giro system referred to in **5.** Each day branches remit bundles of credit transfers to their clearing departments in London and these are handed over to the representatives of the other banks to be dealt with in a similar fashion to cheques (*see* **7** *above*).

9. Computer clearing. The English and Scottish banks established the Bankers' Automated Clearing Services Ltd, which is a company that operates a clearing system based on the use of computers. Instead of preparing transfer vouchers in order to debit the account of one person and credit the account of another, such as the standing orders, direct debits and salary payments referred to in **3, 4** and **5** above, the items are put on to magnetic tapes. They then pass through Bankers' Automated Clearing Services and in effect pass from the paying bank's computer to the receiving bank's computer. It is possible for larger bank customers to transmit information direct to BACS through a telephone link. As the banks have computerised their customers' accounts it is possible for transfers to be made in this fashion and there have been several interesting developments in the use of the technique. Electronic funds transfer (EFT) is already taking place through SWIFT and in the near future EFTPOS (electronic funds transfer at the point of sale) will be in operation. Through this it will be possible for the larger shopkeepers to debit a customer's bank account directly by a computer link.

10. Daily settlement. Each working day it is necessary for the banks to summarise all of the transactions with one another that have resulted from the debit clearing (of the previous day), the credit clearing and the Bankers' Automated Clearing Services. On the daily statement all the balances due from the other banks are listed on the debit side and on the credit side all payments due to other banks are listed. These statements are totalled and the difference between the two sides represents the net balance due from or to all the other banks collectively. All that is then necessary is for the bank's account at the Bank of England to be debited or credited with this sum. Obviously the overall position must be that the total of the debits to clearing bank accounts at the Bank of England must be equal to the credits, and at the end of the day after these transactions have been dealt with nothing is owed by one bank to another in respect of the day's clearing transactions. Several million debit and credit items have changed hands, yet the final settlement amounts to only a few transactions.

11. The Clearing House Automated Payments System (CHAPS). Since February 1984 this system has supplemented the town clearing system through which cheques for more than £10,000 drawn on branches of the banks within the City of London can be cleared on the same day. The member banks of the CHAPS system (the settlement banks) are now able to send funds to one another by electronic means for settlement on the same day and they are also able to send payments as agents for other banks and for their customers. Some of the larger customers have direct computer links and can settle transactions between themselves via a bank's computer and its links with CHAPS.

CASH DISPENSERS AND CHEQUE CARDS

12. Automated teller machines (ATMs). By the end of 1984 the banks will have had more than 6,500 ATMs installed. These are machines installed in the front walls of banks (and conceivably in supermarkets and factories and offices before long) at which customers can draw cash and, usually, check on their balance, order a statement or order a cheque book. Customers are issued with plastic cards for the purpose together with a code number known only to themselves which they can key into the ATM to identify themselves. The building societies are proposing to instal a joint ATM system which is likely to provide up to 1,000 machines for the use of building society customers.

13. Cheque guarantee cards. A customer of a bank who has a cheque guarantee card may cash his cheques up to a maximum of £50 at any other branch or bank, and the card also guarantees payment to any retailer who sells him goods up to that amount. Special cheque cards are now issued to customers for use at banks in Europe. They are accepted as sufficient identification and as a guarantee for the encashment of the card-holder's own cheque up to the £50 limit.

The person who sells goods for which payment is to be made by cheque suported by a cheque guarantee card is guaranteed payment up to the limit specified on the card provided that the drawer signs the cheque in the presence of the payee. The seller must also check that the signature agrees with that on the card, that a proper cheque form of the drawee bank and branch is used, and that the number of the cheque card is written on the back of the cheque by the payee or his agent. The cheque card must not be out of date.

As far as the bank's customer is concerned he must keep the cheque book and card in separate places and must notify the bank if the cheque card is lost. These conditions are laid down in the agreement when the cheque card is issued and repeated when the card is renewed.

Once a cheque has been drawn with the backing of a cheque guaranteed card payment cannot be countermanded, nor can the banker on whom it is drawn refuse to pay it provided that all the terms of the card's use have been completed with.

The customer to whom a cheque card has been issued must not use it to overdraw the account without the prior agreement of the bank and to do so is a criminal offence under the Theft Act 1968 (*R.* v. *Kovacs* (1974) and *R.* v. *Charles* (1976).

PROGRESS TEST 17

1. List the three most common debits to a bank customer's account. **(1)**

2. Describe the sets of figures that appear along the code line of a cheque. **(2)**

3. What are the advantages to the customer in authorising his bank to make standing order payments on his behalf? **(3)**

4. Why might the system of direct debits be preferable to the standing order or credit transfer system as far as the beneficiary is concerned? **(4)**

5. Describe the bank giro and explain its possible advantages and disadvantages over the cheque system. **(5)**

6. Who owns the Bankers' Clearing House and what changes are

about to take place in this connection?   **(6)**

7. Describe how the debit clearing works   **(7)**

8. Describe the credit clearing. What is the fundamental difference between the credit clearing and the debit clearing?   **(8)**

9. What was the purpose of the establishment of the Bankers' Automated Clearing Services Ltd?   **(9)**

10. How do the London Clearing Bankers settle their daily transactions   **(10)**

11. Describe the Clearing House Automated Payments System. **(11)**

12. What is an automated teller machine?   **(12)**

13. What uses can a holder make of a cheque guarantee card? **(13)**

14. What are the rights of the bank, the customer and the payee, when a cheque guarantee card is used?   **(13)**

CHAPTER XVIII

Overseas Banking Services

METHODS OF PAYMENT

1. Interbank balances. Commercial transactions between exporters and importers, and other transactions such as overseas investments, do not involve the movement of actual currencies between countries. Instead, because banks keep balances with other banks abroad, all that is necessary to settle a transaction is to debit the account of one bank and credit that of another. All the British banks keep accounts in foreign currencies with banks overseas and also maintain balances in sterling in the UK for overseas banks. If a customer of Midland Bank therefore wishes to make a payment in French francs for some goods he has imported from Paris, then Midland Bank can instruct, say, Crédit Lyonnais to pay the francs to the French exporter and debit Midland Bank's account in its books. Midland Bank will then debit the customer with the sterling equivalent. Likewise, Crédit Lyonnais will no doubt have payments to make in sterling to British exporters on behalf of its customers, and will instruct Midland Bank (or some other British bank) to debit its sterling account with the amounts involved.

There are a number of ways in which an importer of goods can effect payment through the banking system, but whatever method is used, the result will be either to reduce the foreign currency balance of the importer's bank with a bank overseas or to increase the sterling balances in London of the overseas bank (the exporter's bank). One way is for the importer to ask his bank for a banker's draft. In the example above, the draft would have to be in French francs and the draft would be drawn on Crédit Lyonnais. The draft is in effect a cheque drawn by one bank upon another and when it is paid in by the French exporter to his account with a bank in France it will be debited to the Midland Bank's account with Crédit Lyonnais, thus reducing the stock of French francs.

Banks replenish their foreign currency balances by buying from their cutomers claims upon foreign banks and by buying foreign currency in the foreign exchange market. In this market, banks with excess foreign currency balances sell them at the current market rates of exchange to those other banks in need of them.

2. Bills of exchange. A large proportion of overseas commercial transactions is settled by bills of exchange. A definition of a bill of exchange has already been given in XII and the reader would be wise to refer back to that definition at this stage. The majority of bills used in overseas trade are drawn on banks rather than directly on the importer as in the one illustrated in Fig 3. The drawer is the person who draws the bill (the exporter to whom money is due). The drawee is the person to whom the bill is addressed (the importer's bank or the importer himself) and the payee is the person who is to receive payment. Usually, though by no means always, the drawer and the payee is the same person or firm.

EXCHANGE FOR   £1,000   15th February   19

At   Ninety days after sight   *pay this*   sole·   *Bill of Exchange*
                                                          to the Order of

            ourselves

            ONE THOUSAND POUNDS STERLING

            in part utilisation of your irrevocable credit No. 935790

                                          For and on behalf of
                                          Fabbrica Speciale S/A

To   Dogger Bank Ltd.,
     Overseas Branch, ...
     London.   Director

FIG. 3   *A bill of exchange.*

Bills are usually expressed to be payable one, two, three or six months after date (or sight) or thirty, sixty, ninety or one hundred and eighty days after date (or sight). The date is the date on the bill, but when it is payable at so many days after sight the date of sight is the date it is presented for acceptance.

As we saw in XII the drawee's acceptance of a bill is necessary before he is legally liable on the bill. He signifies his acceptance (he undertakes to pay it on the due date) by writing his name across the face of the bill. This provides the exporter with a negotiable instrument which he can either turn into cash immediately or hold on to until the date of maturity. If he wants the cash before the due date of the bill he can either negotiate the bill or ask his bank for an advance against the collection of it. The negotiation of the bill involves selling it to a bank at the face value less discount. The bank then collects the proceeds on maturity in its own right. The bank may be prepared to give the exporter an advance against the future proceeds of the bill if it is to collect the bill for the customer. By taking the bill for collection it is simply acting as the exporter's agent sending the bill (and possibly documents relating to the goods concerned) to a correspondent bank overseas, with a request that it presents the bills for acceptance (if necessary) and for payment, and that it remits the proceeds back to the exporter's bank.

A bill of exchange may be either a clean bill, i.e. it has no documents attached, or a documentary bill. Documentary bills, as the name suggests, are bills accompanied by the documents of title to the goods. The exporter sends the documents through his bank for delivery to the importer upon acceptance of the accompanying bill of exchange (a D/A bill, i.e. documents against acceptance) or upon payment of the bill (a D/P bill, i.e. documents against payment).

There is a set of international rules concerning the collection of bills by the banks for their customers entitled *Uniform Rules for Collections*. These were drawn up by the International Chamber of Commerce in conjunction with the banks and the British banks have agreed to work to them. Although the rules are merely a code of conduct and not legally enforceable, there is little doubt that a court would decide in favour of a bank which had collected a bill within the terms of the rules and had made it clear to its customer from the outset that the bill was to be collected under the rules. In fact the banks print a clause in the customer's form of instruction to the bank to this effect.

3. Documentary credits. Where an exporter is able to persuade the buyer to open a documentary credit in his favour he receives a bank's undertaking to accept, and/or pay, a bill of exchange drawn on it for the value of the goods, or possibly to make an immediate payment for the goods without a bill being drawn. The following precise definition of a documentary credit is taken from the *Uniform Customs and Practice for Documentary Credits* (1974 revision) which is an international code, also drawn up by the International Chamber of Commerce, that the British banks work to.

"Any arrangement, however named or described, whereby a bank (the issuing bank), acting at the request and in accordance with the instructions of a customer (the applicant for the credit), is to make payment to or to the order of a third party (the beneficiary) or is to pay, accept or negotiate bills of exchange (drafts) drawn by the beneficiary, or authorises such payments to be made or such drafts to be paid, accepted or negotiated by another bank, against stipulated documents, provided that the term and conditions of the credit are complied with."

It is thus an arrangement between an importer and his bank, the bank being willing to pledge itself by way of a letter of credit addressed to the exporter (the beneficiary) to make a payment provided that the documents relating to the goods are in order. In as much as the documents will be handled by the banks concerned, the issuing bank will have some control over the goods and may be able to ensure that the proceeds of the resale of them are used to repay the bank if there are insufficient other funds on the importer's account. The exporter hands over the documents to the bank in his country (i.e. the correspondent bank selected by the issuing bank which may or may not be the exporter's bank, or the issuing bank itself if it is located in the exporter's country). He will then have his bill of exchange accepted or paid according to the terms of the letter of credit and the documents pass from the correspondent bank to the issuing bank.

A documentary credit may be a confirmed credit, i.e. one to which a bank in the exporter's country has added its undertaking that the terms of the credit will be fulfilled. It may also be revocable or irrevocable. A revocable credit offers no real protection to the exporter, in that it may be cancelled at any time, whereas the terms of an irrevocable credit cannot be altered, nor can the credit be cancelled, without the agreement of all the parties to it.

The main documents called for in a documentary credit are the invoice, the bill of lading (or other transport document) and the insurance policy or certificate. The invoice will usually specify the quality as well as the quantity of the goods and the price being charged, and several copies may be called for in the credit. A bill of lading is the document of title to the goods and the goods are handed over only against the surrender of the bill of lading. It certifies that the goods have been received on board ship for transportation and delivery. The insurance policy or certificate covers the transit of the goods by sea. If a consignment is covered by a general policy covering a series of consignments an insurance certificate is usually issued instead of a policy.

Other documents that may be called for in a documentary credit are a railway receipt, an air consignment note, a certificate of origin and a certificate of quality. The first two of these would be used in place of a bill of lading if the goods were being transported by rail or air respectively instead of by sea.

4. Telegraphic and mail transfers. A telegraphic transfer is an instruction from a bank in one country to a bank overseas requesting it to transfer some of the balance on the instructing bank's account to the person named on the transfer. A British importer, for instance, will ask his bank to make such a transfer through a bank in the exporter's country. The exporter will be credited with a sum in his own currency (which will be deducted from the British bank's account) and the importer will be debited by his bank with the sterling equivalent plus expenses. This is the most speedy form of payment because it is telegraphic, but it is more expensive than the slower alternative of a mail transfer. The latter is similar to a telegraphic transfer but the advice to the bank overseas is sent by mail (invariably airmail these days). To a considerable extent the telegraphic transfer has been replaced by SWIFT (Society for Worldwide Interbank Financial Telecommunication), a system of telecommunications set up by a large number of British and overseas banks. Member banks are able to send instructions to one another through this closed system and obviate the need for sending messages by cable through the Post Office, which involves using an identification code.

5. Banker's drafts and cheques. Banker's drafts have already been referred to in **1** *above*. A banker's draft is a cheque drawn by one bank on another, and like an ordinary cheque it is an instruction to the bank on whom it is drawn to transfer some of the drawer's balance to another person.

An importer may wish to settle his account with the exporter by simply drawing a cheque on his bank in the same way that he would if he were settling an inland transaction. This method has several disadvantages, however. Firstly it may be in contravention of exchange control regulations (in the UK, for instance, before Exchange Control was lifted in 1980 it was illegal to pay in this way unless the cheque had an official stamp of approval by the British bank and the appropriate exchange control forms had been completed if they were required). From the exporter's point of view the cheque is not a very satisfactory method of payment because he has the problem of having to send the cheque to his bank for collection and this is a time-consuming and costly process.

6. Speed, safety and convenience. The methods of payment mentioned above need to be looked at in terms of speed, safety and convenience.

The most satisfactory arrangement for the exporter, and which would satisfy all three criteria, would be payment in advance by telegraphic transfer or SWIFT. However, whereas this may be practicable for small consignments to be sent by post it is unlikely that imports of any size would be paid for in this way. A confirmed irrevocable documentary credit is the next best thing. The exporter can by this means ensure that he receives payment immediately upon shipment. Provided that he has taken steps to get all the necessary documents and complied with all the terms of the credit there is no risk, as he has an undertaking by a bank to pay. It is also a method which is convenient to him.

To the importer, a documentary credit is also a satisfactory method of settlement, though perhaps not as satisfactory as it is to the exporter. The importer would prefer not to pay until he has received the goods and possibly resold them. The safety aspect which he will be most concerned with will be whether or not the goods will be up to the required standard when they arrive. He must do his best to ensure that the quality is clearly specified in his contract with the supplier, but the description of the goods in the documentary credit must be a simple one which will not require the banks concerned to examine the references to quality too closely. The importer can protect himself further by requiring that the goods are examined by someone in the exporter's country with expert knowledge of the product, who will sign a certificate of quality which must accompany the other documents relating to the goods. As far as convenience is concerned, the opening of a documentary credit does provide a means whereby the documents of title can be channelled through to him, having been checked against the list of his requirements contained in the credit.

The safety aspect is also important as far as the two banks are concerned, the exporter's bank and the importer's bank. The exporter's bank may have lent him money to finance the production of the goods and will have the satisfaction of knowing that payment will be forthcoming upon shipment if a documentary credit has been opened in the exporter's favour. The importer's bank will have undertaken to make the payment under the documentary credit and will therefore wish to keep close control of the documents of title to the goods, releasing them only when it is satisfied that the proceeds of resale will be received into the importer's account.

When exporters and importers have been trading with one another over a period of years they will have built up confidence between them to the point where documentary credits are no longer considered necessary. The ultimate development would be to trade on open account, i.e. for the exporter to ship the goods and send the documents direct to the buyer. A payment would then be made at some agreed future date by bill of exchange, telegraphic or mail transfer or banker's draft. This is similar to the way in which transactions are normally conducted on the home market.

Between the two extremes of a documentary credit on the one hand and trading on open account on the other, lies the system of documentary bills of exchange. These provide some security through control of the documents until acceptance or payment of the bill, but it is a slower method. It is less convenient to both parties than trading on open account, but the system does offer the convenience of being able to obtain bank finance on the strength of the bill of exchange and the accompanying documents.

OTHER OVERSEAS SERVICES

7. Services to exporters. In addition to providing the methods of payment considered above and lending money to exporters in anticipation of the receipt of such payments, the banks provide other services to exporters. These include the following:

(*a*) Information about business opportunities abroad, by carrying out research into the potential demand for particular products.
(*b*) Economic and political reports on the countries with which the exporter intends to trade.
(*c*) Status reports on particular overseas buyers.
(*d*) Information on trade and exchange restrictions in the countries concerned.

8. Services to importers. Banking services to importers also go beyond the provision of the methods of payment and of finance. They include the following:

(*a*) Information about sources of supply and the names of potential foreign suppliers.
(*b*) Status enquires on individual suppliers.
(*c*) Information concerning UK import controls which at present are of course very few.

9. Services to travellers. Before travelling abroad on business or for pleasure, customers (and to some extent non-customers) of the banks may obtain their foreign currency requirements and traveller's cheques and may also make arrangements with correspondent banks abroad to obtain payments in foreign currency as required. When travelling to the Continent they may obtain a Euro-cheque card which will enable them to cash their own cheques at overseas banks.

PROGRESS TEST 18

1. Do transactions with other countries involve the movement of cash? **(1)**

2. How do international banks settle transactions between themselves? **(1)**

3. How do banks replenish their holdings of foreign currencies? **(1)**

4. Define a bill of exchange. **(2)**

5. What is meant by the acceptance of a bill of exchange? **(2)**

6. Define (*a*) negotiation and (*b*) collection of a bill of exchange. **(2)**

7. Distinguish between a clean bill and a documentary bill. **(2)**

8. What are D/A and D/P bills? **(2)**

9. What is a documentary credit? **(3)**

10. Define (*a*) confirmed (*b*) revocable (*c*) irrevocable documentary credits. **(3)**

11. What are the main documents called for in a documentary credit? **(3)**

12. Distinguish between a telegraphic transfer and a mail transfer. **(4)**

13. What is meant by SWIFT? **(4)**

14. What is a banker's draft? **(5)**

15. Can bank customers use ordinary cheques for international payments? **(5)**

16. What are the relative advantages and disadvantages of each method of payment available to foreign traders? **(6)**

17. What other overseas services do banks provide for exporters? **(7)**

18. What other overseas services do banks provide for importers? **(8)**

19. What are the banking services available to travellers? **(9)**

CHAPTER XIX

Other Banking Services

THE HANDLING OF CASH

1. Settling transactions. So far in this book we have considered three of the most important banking services: the acceptance of deposits, the provisions of payments mechanisms (both inland and overseas) and the provision of credit. All three of these are very much interrelated, as the payments mechanisms so often put into effect the arrangements made to borrow money from the banks, i.e. the customer draws a cheque or arranges for a payment to be made to an overseas supplier to incur an overdraft which the bank has agreed to provide. The overdraft may create fresh deposits and the payments mechanisms will be used to transfer the ownership of bank deposits in the settlement of transactions.

A fourth vital function is also concerned with the settling of transactions; this is the provision of notes and coin in the right denominations and at the right time. The handling of notes and coin is an expensive and time-consuming service, a fact which is not always recognised by those who avail themselves of the service. The firm which has to prepare the wage packets for its workers each week would be very surprised if it found that it could not collect the money from the bank in the precise denominations so carefully worked out by the wages clerk in advance. There are times when there is a local shortage of a particular coin but this is unusual and only temporary. The service is one which benefits both customers and non-customers of the banks, for anyone who handles notes and coin—which means everyone—is able to take advantage of a system that ensures that cash is moved around the country smoothly and efficiently.

2. The distribution of cash. Some branches of the banks take in more notes and coin than they need, while for others the reverse applies. For a few branches the inflow and outflow of cash is evenly balanced and only occasional movements of notes and coin are required.

The cash situation for a particular branch will depend a great deal upon its location and hence the type of customers that predominate. A branch in Oxford Street is likely to take in more notes and coin than it requires, because the shops will be its main customers. A branch on or near an industrial estate would probably have to provide more notes and coin for the industrial firms' wages than it took across the counter. Another important factor is seasonal trade. For instance, a branch near a seafront in a holiday town will find the flow of cash rather different in the summer than in the winter, and the flow of cash in a shopping area is very much greater at Christmas time.

Each branch must determine its future cash requirements on the basis of past experience and this is a skill which has to be learnt. Unexpected heavy demands for cash can usually be met by summoning the help of nearby branches and other banks but, generally speaking, requirements can usually be anticipated and provided for in advance.

In addition to making sure that it has sufficient notes and coin of the right denominations, a branch bank also has the task of withdrawing old and dirty notes and worn coins and replacing them with new or serviceable ones. Cashiers sort notes into clean and dirty bundles and the old notes are sent to the Bank of England for destruction. New notes are acquired by the Head Office of the banks from the Bank of England and distributed to branches.

The banks have bullion departments with vans and local distribution centres and are responsible for much of the carriage of notes and coin. The banks also use the services of the security companies and to some extent use the postal service for the despatch of notes. There are also local arrangements between branches and other banks whereby branches with surplus cash meet the needs of other branches that have insufficient paid into them. The banks insure notes and coin in transit either with insurance companies or through their own insurance schemes.

3. Night safes and cash dispensers. For business customers, especially retailers, who have appreciable amounts of cash at the end of the day after the banks have closed, the banks provide night safe wallets which can be deposited in the night safe at any time after the bank is closed. The customer locks his cash and cheques in the wallet and places it in the safe by unlocking the trap that is built into the front wall of the bank. The next day he is able to collect the wallet at the counter and pay in the contents or he can permit the bank to open the wallet on his behalf.

To make cash available to the customer at times when the bank is closed, the banks have automated teller machines built into the front of many of their branches (*see* XVII, **12.**)

INVESTMENT SERVICES

4. Stock Exchange transactions. The banks place orders with stockbrokers on behalf of customers to buy and sell Stock Exchange securities. The banks now charge for this service and also share the normal stockbroker's commission which is charged to customers together with the stamp duty. Reports from stockbrokers on the desirability or otherwise of investing in particular stocks and shares are obtained for customers, but normally a bank manager would not give his own advice on the matter. He would furnish details of the yields to be obtained from investing in the various forms of national savings and purchase and obtain repayment of them for customers. He may also obtain details of various other investment schemes from the bank's investment department. Deposits with building societies will also be made for customers.

5. Investment management. Whereas local managers would not expect to give investment advice, it is possible for a customer to hand over the management of his investments completely to the bank. The customer has to give the bank written authority to buy and sell securities on his behalf and the investment department will supervise the customer's holdings of stocks and shares in an endeavour to ensure that they are managed in his best interests.

6. Safe custodies. The bank customer is able to deposit his stock and share certificates, deeds and other important documents with the bank for safe-keeping. He may have a box or parcel placed in the strongroom for safe-keeping.

In some of the larger branches, special safe deposit compartments are made available to customers. The customer has the key to the compartment and has direct access to it, whereas with normal safe custody facilities it is necessary to ask at the counter for the box, parcel or document to be brought out of the safe.

7. New issues. Where a company issues stocks and shares on the Stock Exchange, the registrar's department of a bank or the bank's subsidiary merchant bank may become involved. The bank may receive applications for the shares from the public and will be responsible for alloting these and keeping a register of the shareholders.

INFORMATION SERVICES

8. Status reports. A customer may give his bank as a reference if he is embarking on some transaction which involves credit, e.g. he signs a hire-purchase contract. The bank will then give a guarded report on his creditworthiness. Likewise, the customer may ask his bank to obtain a status report on a person or firm he is intending to deal with and may ask for this to be brought up to date at set intervals. The banks keep reports on hundreds of thousands of firms and individuals and exchange information with other banks. They also use the services of the large credit information agencies.

9. Economic intelligence. The economic intelligence departments and overseas departments of the banks study developments in the economy, in individual industries and in overseas countries and are able to provide information to customers on request. They also produce reviews and other publications on various subjects.

Advice and information is also available from branch managers who have a wide experience of financial and other matters as well as a knowledge of local affairs.

EXECUTORSHIP AND INCOME TAX

10. Executor and trustee department. The work of this department of a bank is to act as excutor and possibly trustee for a customer upon his death. By appointing the bank to fulfil this task, the customer knows that his wishes will be carried out by experts, and with impartiality. His relatives, or possibly a friend, are relieved of a task which can be burdensome especially at a time of distress.

11. Income tax. As an alternative to appointing an accountant to do the work, a customer can employ his bank's income tax department to look after his tax's affairs. In doing so he may save himself money as the department will be fully conversant with the tax allowances that can be claimed. They will complete his tax returns and assessments and claim any refunds that are due to him.

MARKETING BANKING SERVICES

12. The marketing department. Each of the large banks has a marketing department which is responsible for the collection and interpretation of data concerning the markets and competition for the bank's services. The department works with other departments of the bank to ensure that collectively they are achieving the best possible promotion of their services. They monitor results to see how they compare with the targets set. As the banks are selling services rather than goods the benefits to the purchaser are not so obvious and it takes time for him to fully appreciate these benefits. It may therefore take some time for the bank to fully assess the success or otherwise of any new service they have promoted.

The banks have an Inter-Bank Research Organisation which looks into the need for such services as the Clearing House Automated Payments System (CHAPS) which are run on a mutual basis, and this organisation also produces data on which the individual banks can base the introduction of services on a competitive basis.

Much of a bank's marketing is in fact done at the counter where the clerk or cashier acts as the marketor in selling the bank's services to the customer, who may have seen in a newspaper an advertisement inserted by the marketing department. The attitude and knowledge of the person on the counter is obviously vitally important when it comes to convincing the customer that he should buy the service.

PROGRESS TEST 19

1. Why is the movement of notes and coin by the banks so important **(1)**

2. What causes one branch of a bank to have a surplus of notes and coin while another needs to acquire additional cash? **(2)**

3. How do the banks distribute notes and coin? **(2)**

4. Who is responsible for sorting out and disposing of dirty bank notes? **(2)**

5. How does the night safe system help the local retailers? **(3)**

6. What is an ATM? **(3)**

7. Describe the investment services that a bank offers a customer. **(4, 5, 6)**

8. Explain the work of a bank in connection with a company's share issue. **(7)**

9. What are status reports? **(8)**

10. Explain briefly the types of advice and information the banks are able to give. **(9)**

11. Describe the work of the executor and trustee department of a bank. **(10)**

12. What are the advantages of appointing a bank's income tax department to look after personal tax affairs? **(11)**

13. What is meant by the marketing of banking services? Who performs this function? **(12)**

Examination Technique

The student preparing for the BTEC National Certificate or Diploma or Bankers Conversion Course Elements of Banking examination can expect a three-hour paper and a possible choice of, say, five out of nine or ten questions. He will therefore have about thirty-five minutes to answer each question and in that time would be expected to write an essay-type answer or, possibly, complete some other form of assignment. Sometimes in BTEC examinations the three hours is devoted to one large project split into a number of parts. In essay-type questions a straight list of facts will not do; the student must put them in a logical order and in such a way that they form a smooth-flowing essay.

Always bear in mind the following general points before tackling any examination question.

(*a*) *Read the question very carefully*, to ensure that you know precisely what is required. An answer to a question which has not been asked will earn no marks at all, even though it may be correct in every detail. Some questions are carefully phrased to assess the candidate's ability to think and to decide which points are involved.

(*b*) *Read the question a second time,* and prepare a rough list of the points that need to be covered. Only the briefest amount of detail is required. For example in answering the question "What factors determine the uses which a commercial bank makes of money deposited with it?" the following points would probably occur to you: responsibility to shareholders to make profit, advances ratio, need for liquidity, reserve requirements, flow of maturing assets, need for premises, need to diversify.

(*c*) *Arrange the points in a logical sequence.* Thus in the question above you might decide to put the points in the following order.

   (*i*) Responsibility to shareholders to make a profit.
  (*ii*) Need for liquidity.
 (*iii*) Flow of maturing assets.
 (*iv*) Reserve requirements.
  (*v*) Advances ratio.

(*vi*) Need to diversify.
(*vii*) Need for premises.

It is essential to have your points in a logical order in this way, for the examiner can then see that you are capable of thinking out the answer and of writing an essay in which one point leads to another. You may also avoid confusing and even contradicting yourself!

(*d*) *Write your answer in the form of an essay,* not in the form of numbered notes. There are very few exceptions to this rule, but possibly the examiner might ask you to list, for instance, the functions of a central bank with brief comments on each. However, unless it is clearly stipulated in the question that such a list is required, you are safe to assume that an essay is required and you should develop your answer in that fashion.

(*e*) *Use good phraseology and write neatly with a good pen.*

SPECIMEN QUESTION
What are the *main* assets and liabilities of a commercial bank? Describe these and relate them to the services which such a bank provides.

ROUGH NOTES
(1) Main liabilities, capital and deposits; (2) description of deposits; (3) cash in hand—provision of cash as required by customers; (4) liquid assets, call money, Treasury bills, other bills; (5) ability to repay deposits; (6) cheques in course of collection— provision of payments mechanism; (7) advances.

MODEL ANSWER
The two main liabilities that appear on the balance sheet of a commercial bank are Capital and Reserve and Deposits. The first of these reflects the fact that the bank is a public company and has shareholders. The total nominal value of these shares appears under the heading of Capital and any undistributed profits under Reserves. The second liability, Deposits, represents all the balances held by the bank on behalf of its customers whether on current account, deposit account or term deposit. The acceptance of deposits is a service which banks must provide if they are to function, for they produce an income by taking deposits and lending them in a variety of ways.

On the asset side of the balance sheet the first item is Cash in Hand and Balances at the Bank of England. An important function of a bank is to provide its customers with the notes and coin they need at the right time, in the right place and in the denominations they require. By keeping cash in the tills and balances at the Bank of

England which can be drawn upon at any time (apart from the $\frac{1}{2}$ per cent non-operational account balance), the bank is able to fulfil this function.

Cash is a liquid asset and together with Call Money, Treasury Bills and Other Bills, it forms the group of assets which are either cash or can easily be turned into cash. These liquid assets are held to ensure that the bank can meet its depositors' claims for repayment. It is not likely that a large commercial bank's customers would all demand repayment within a short period so that the bank can safely keep only a modest proportion of its deposits (about 20 per cent) in these liquid assets. The item Other Bills consists of bills of exchange which the bank has discounted for its customers (i.e. bought from them at a discount on the face value) and thus reflects a further service which the bank provides.

In addition to the three services already mentioned in looking at the assets and liabilities of a bank, i.e. the acceptance of deposits, the provision of notes and coin and discounting bills, there are two other services which are revealed by looking at the bank's balance sheet. These are the provision of payments mechanisms and the provision of credit. The first of these is reflected in the item Cheques in Course of Collection and Balances with Other Banks and the other is the item Advances.

Cheques on other banks paid in by customers are sent for collection through the London Clearing House and the value of those going through this process will be shown under this heading. So, too, will balances kept for convenience with other banks. The importance of the cheque system is to some extent indicated by the fact that at any one time the total of this asset in the balance sheet of a major bank might amount to £500 million. Also allowed for in this item will be the value of items that are passing through the credit clearing (the Bank Giro) at a particular time. Unlike cheques, these are sums of money due to be paid over to other banks and will have had to be deducted from the amount due from other banks for the cheques in course of collection.

By the provision of credit through loans, overdrafts and term loans, the banks provide a vital service, primarily to trade and industry, but to private individuals as well. Without this capital, industry would not have been able to develop in the way it has. The banks lend approximately 70 per cent of their depositors' money by way of advances, making this the largest of the assets on the balance sheet.

Test Papers

Do not attempt these papers until you have thoroughly mastered the relevant parts of the book, and the appropriate Progress Tests. Do each paper under strict examination conditions, bearing in mind the hints on exam technique given in Appendix I. When you have completed a test, check your answers with the aid of the text references.

Allow three hours for each paper; all questions carry equal marks. Answer five questions.

TEST PAPER 1
Money and Credit

1. Describe the way in which the system of barter gave way to indirect exchange. Explain why precious metals became the most acceptable forms of money. (I, **1–4**)

2. What are the functions of money? Explain why money is so vital in a free society. (I, **5–9**)

3. Describe the development of both coins and paper money in Britain up to the First World War. (II, **1–8**)

4. What is the fiduciary issue? Describe the enactments that have controlled its size. Does it matter that the note issue is now forty times as large as in 1928? (II, **7**)

5. Describe the origin of the cheque and its importance in the development of Deposit Banking. (III, **1–2**)

6. What constitutes our present-day money supply? Briefly explain the two different ways of measuring it. (III, **5**)

7. What constitutes a "near-money" asset and what distinguishes it from money? Give examples of "near-money". (III, **4**)

TEST PAPER 2
Savings Institutions

1. What is meant by savings and why are they so important in a modern community? (IV, **1–3**)

2. Distinguish between the two meanings of the term investment. Describe the main types of capital investment. (IV, **4–5**)

3. Describe the development and services of the National Savings Bank. (V, **2**)

4. Explain the importance of assurance companies and pension funds as channels for savings. (V, **5**)

5. Discuss the importance of the commercial banks in attracting personal savings. (V, **15–18**)

6. Distinguish between a unit trust and an investment trust. (V, **12, 13**)

7. Describe the role of the building societies in the national economy. What tax privileges do they and their members receive? (V, **9, 10**)

TEST PAPER 3
The British Banking System

1. Describe the history and development of the Bank of England. (VI, **1–6**)

2. Briefly describe each of the present-day functions of the Bank of England. (VI, **7–15**)

3. Describe the main Acts of Parliament which influenced the development of the commercial banks in Britain in the nineteenth century. (VII, **1–3**)

4. What major developments have occurred in commercial banking in the twentieth century? (VII, **4**)

5. Distinguish between a clearing bank and a merchant bank. (VII, **6**)

6. Describe the development and functions of the Trustee Savings Banks. (VII, **7–10**)

7. Explain the interrelationships between the Bank of England, the discount houses and the commercial banks. (VIII, **4–7**)

TEST PAPER 4
The Legal Background

1. Explain briefly the contractual relationships between banker and customer. (XI, **1–5**)

2. Identify unauthorised acts by agents and their effects on a bank. (XI, **14**)

3. What is the significance of a crossing on a cheque? Explain the difference between a general crossing and a specific crossing. (XII, **12**)

4. Explain the provisions of the Cheques Act 1957. (XII, **13**)

5. Explain the meaning of the term "negotiable" and give some examples of negotiable instruments. (XII, **1**)

6. Explain the responsibilities of the parties to a bill of exchange. (XII, **7**)

TEST PAPER 5
Commercial Banks' Sources and Uses of Funds

1. With reference to the main assets and liabilities of a commercial bank, describe how it strikes a balance between profitability and liquidity. (XIII, **1–15**)

2. Describe the reserve assets and eligible liabilities of a bank. (XIII, **17, 18**)

3. Outline the purposes of and the methods employed for official control of bank credit. (VI, **19–22**, X **3–5**)

4. Outline the concept of deposit insurance and assess its significance. (XII, **21**)

5. Explain the significance of certificates of deposit. Why might they appear on both the liabilities and the assets side of a bank balance sheet? (XIII, **9**)

6. Explain what is meant by cheques in course of collection in a bank balance sheet. Is this a liquid asset? (XIII, **8**)

7. What is meant by monetary policy and who is responsible for its implementation? (X, **1**)

TEST PAPER 6
The Purposes of Bank Lending

1. Explain what is meant by the term "self-liquidating advances" and give some examples of these. (XIV, **1**)

2. In what ways have the banks become involved in longer-term lending in recent years? (XIV, **3–8**)

3. Explain the ways in which interest on bank advances is calculated. (XIV, **10**)

4. What is meant by post-shipment finance? Describe the incentives given to the banks to increase this type of lending. (XIV, **7, 8**)

5. Describe each of the following terms.
(*a*) Bank overdraft.
(*b*) Bank loan.
(*c*) Personal instalment loan.
(*d*) Term loan.
(XIV, **2–4**)

6. Explain the various factors that a bank manager must take into account in deciding whether or not to agree to a request for an advance. (XV, **1–9**)

7. In what ways will sets of final accounts be helpful to a bank which is considering an application for a substantial advance by a business customer? (XVI, **1–8**)

TEST PAPER 7
Methods of Payment and Other Bank Services

1. Define in detail the main items that are debited to a bank customer's account. (XVII, 1–4)

2. Describe the Bank Giro system. (XVII, 5)

3. Give an account of the Bank Clearing House and how cheques and credits are cleared. (XVII, 6–11)

4. Briefly describe how a bill of exchange with or without a documentary credit can be used as a means of making a payment through the banking system to a person or firm overseas. (XVIII, 2–3)

5. Analyse from the aspects of speed, safety and convenience, the various methods of making a payment overseas through the banking system. (XVIII, 2–6)

6. Describe the function of the banks in collecting and re-distributing cash within a local community. (XIX, 1–3)

7. The main functions of a bank are to accept deposits, provide payments mechanisms and provide credit. Describe some of the other services they provide to their customers. (XIX, 1–11)

Business and Technician Education Council Elements of Banking Modules Reading Index

LEARNING OBJECTIVES: ELEMENTS OF BANKING 1

		Section Reference(s)
A1	Briefly trace the evolution of money, identifying its functions and the characteristics required of whatever is used as money to to perform its functions satisfactorily.	I, **1–9** II, **1–7**
A2	Identify the shortcomings of money as an indicator of value and outline methods of protecting its value.	I, **8** X, **1–6**
A3	Distinguish the forms that money takes in a modern society (coinage, notes, legal tender, bank deposits).	II, **8** III, **3, 5**
A4	Distinguish between money and "near money".	III, **4**
B1	Outline briefly the origins and development of the UK banking system.	III, **1–2** VI, **1–2** VII, **1–4**
B2	Briefly outline the development of the Bank England, explaining its functions and including its role under the 1979 Banking Act.	VI, **1–15, 19–22**
B3	Distinguish between the short-term money markets, the loan and savings markets and the capital markets (including the Stock Exchange.	VII, **6–14** VIII, **1–6** IX, **1–6**

Section
Reference(s)

D2   Identify and compare major forms of saving   V, **1–18**
(including banks, building societies, pension
funds, insurance companies, unit trusts,
National Savings) and their relative attractiveness to savers.

D3   Specify the principal institutions which on-   V, **1–18**
lend savings and their respective roles in the
economy (banks, buildings societies, finance
houses etc.).

E1   Define the meaning and role of the rate of   V, **16**
interest.   X, **3**

E2   Identify the factors which influence interest   V, **10**
rates.   X, **1–6**

E3   Describe the structure of interest rates   XIV, **10**
including base rates, LIBOR, blue chip etc.

E4   Appreciate in outline the effects of interest   X, **1–6**
rate changes on banking business (domestic
and international), competition for savings,
investment and employment.

F1   Distinguish different types of bank customer   XI, **6–14**
and the different considerations which may
apply to them, with particular reference to
personal and corporate accounts including
executor, trustee, church, club etc.

F2   Understand the basic contractual relation-   XI, **1–14**
ship between banker and customer (e.g.
debtor–creditor, agent–principal) with a
basic understanding of the contractual
capacity of different types of customer
(including provisions related to limited
companies).

F3   Explain the procedure for opening bank   XI, **6–14**

Section
Reference(s)

accounts and the main terms used in mandates and powers of attorney for operating bank accounts and in other bank documents whereby the customer gives instructions to the bank.

F4   Fully appreciate the bank's legal duties   XI, 1–5
     to the customer, e.g. secrecy, acting with
     due care.

F5   Differentiate between joint and several   XI, 8–15
     liability.

G1   Identify the different types of negotiable   XII, 1
     instruments and their particular character-
     istics.

G2   Trace the development of a cheque as a   XII, 10
     method of payment.   XVII, 2

G3   Appreciate the origins and current meanings   XII, 12
     of crossings on cheques.

G4   Explain the responsibility and rights of   XII, 1–15
     parties to cheques and bills of exchange.

G5   Explain the rights of banker, customer and   XVII, 13
     holder of a cheque in the event of misuse of
     a cheque card.

G6   Identify and explain the consequences of   XI, 5
     conversion.   XII, 15

G7   Describe conversion in respect of items held   XI, 5
     in safe custody.

G8   Identify unauthorised acts by agents and   XI, 14
     their effects on the bank.

H1   Identify the different inland methods of   XVII, 1–11
     payment (including cheque, bank giro,

banker's order, direct debit etc.) and explain how they are processed.

H2   Explain the operation of the bank clearing   XVII, **6–11**
      system.

H3   Outline the methods of making international   XVIII, **1–6**
      payments including mail and cable transfers,
      bankers' drafts and the settlement of sterling
      and currency payments between banks.

LEARNING OBJECTIVES: ELEMENTS OF BANKING 2

A1   Outline the link between the money supply   X, **1–6**
      and the level of bank and economic activity.

A2   Identify and evaluate the difference between   III, **5**
      various money aggregates, in particular
      those used for official control purposes.

A3   Appreciate the factors which bring about   X, **1–6**
      changes in the money supply, including
      private and public sector borrowing and
      external factors.

B1   Identify the broad objectives of government   X, **1–6**
      economic policy and the role of monetary
      policy as one of the methods of achieving
      those objectives.

B2   Identify the different techniques available   X, **1–6**
      for implementing monetary policy—money
      aggregates, ratios, interest rates, special
      deposits, quantitative controls, suggestion
      and request.

B3   Be aware of the effects of monetary policy   X, **1–6**
      techniques on the banks.

B4   Distinguish between short-term and long-   X, **1–6**

term interest rates and appreciate the role
of the Government in influencing interest
rates.

B5   Appreciate the relationships between bal-   X, 1–6
     ance of payments, exchange rates and
     interest rates.

C1   Identify the wholesale money markets, their   V, 8
     origins and functions (local authority, inter- VII, 10–14
     bank, company funds, certificates of deposit,
     Eurocurrency markets and the financial
     future market).

C2   Evaluate their role in the economy.   V 8   VII, 10–14

D1   Identify and outline the main services offered   XIV, 2–4
     by the commercial banks to personal cus-   XVII, 1–13
     tomers (e.g. executor and trustee services,   XVIII, 9
     credit cards, hire purchase, insurance etc.).   XIX, 1–11

D2   Identify and outline the main services   XIV, 1–8
     offered by the commercial banks or their   XV, 19
     subsidiaries to business customers (e.g.   XVI, 1–8
     factoring, leasing etc.).   XVII, 1–5, 9, 11
                                              XVIII, 1–9

D3   Relate the range of services to the needs   XIV, 1–8
     of specific types of customer—importers   XV, 19–24
     exporters, manufacturers, retailers, profes-   XVII, 1–13
     sions, householders, students etc.).   XVIII, 1–9
                                              XIX, 1–11

D4   Evaluate the methods adopted by banks for   XIX, 12
     marketing their services.

D5   Recognise the constraints imposed upon   XV, 24
     banks by legislation such as the Consumer
     Credit Act and the Fair Trading Act.

E1   Identify the general principles governing   XV, 1–9
     bank lending and its supervision.

Section
Reference(s)

E2 Identify the various forms of bank lending   XIV, **1–9**
and their suitability for the purposes of
different borrowers.

E3 Outline the special features of contractual   XV, **20–23**
capacity that a banker needs to bear in mind
in lending to minors, executors, house
buyers, sole traders, partnerships and limited
companies.

E4 Identify the circumstances in which security   XV, **9–23**
may be required.

E5 Appreciate the various types and attributes   XV, **10–19**
of security, e.g. land, stocks and shares, life
policies, guarantees.

F1 Explain the liability of banks to persons   XI, **1–5, 14**
affected by their activities, e.g. through   XII, **1–15**
negligence, breach of contract, vicarious
liability, conversion, defamation.

F2 Differentiate between lien, hypothecation   XV, **10–11**
and pledge, and understand the meaning of
safe custody.

F3 Outline the nature of wills, the appointment   XI, **10**
and duties of personal representatives and   XV, **21**
the duties of trustees.

G1 Interpret the final accounts and other   XVI, **1–9**
financial statements of a business from the
viewpoint of profitability, efficiency, liquidity, capital structure and investment.

G2 Interpret the account of a company on the   XVI, **1–9**
basis of a "going" and "gone" concern
through examination of the trading and
profit and loss accounts and the balance
sheet.

G3 Identify the significance of the data relating   XVI, **1–9** to stock (retail and manufacturing), debtors, creditors, borrowing, dividends and tax.

G4   Determine relevant factors relating to cyclical business, off balance sheet finance, plant and machinery, employees etc.   XVI, **1–9**

G5   Understand and apply elementary accounting ratios and appreciate the importance of the cash flow position   XVI, **1–9**

H1   Define the concept of negotiability and relate it to banking instruments.   XII, **1–15**

H2   Explain the meaning of acceptance, endorsement and discharge.   XII, **4**

H3   Name the principal statutes relating to negotiable instruments and outline in general terms their fundamental consequences.   XII, **1–15**

H4   Describe the statutory protection for a holder for value, a holder in due course, the rights and duties of parties to a bill, presentation for acceptance and presentation for payment.   XII, **1–15**

H5   State the position of the collecting banker and the paying banker with regard to statutory protection, negligence, negotiability and endorsement necessary to transfer.   XII, **1–15**

H6   Explain the banker's position in the event of revocation of authority, material alteration and forgery.   XII, **1–15**

H7   Identify the action following the dishonour of a bill of exchange or the non-payment of a cheque.   XII, **1–15**

J1   Identify evidence of ownership, e.g. land   XV, **10–19** certificate and title deeds, and means of checking title.

J2 Outline special factors concerning land   XV, **10–19**
    ownership—freehold/leasehold, registered/
    unregistered, prior charges and interests.

J3 Outline the obligations of mortgagor and   XV, **10–19**
    mortgagee.

J4 Describe the appropriate instruments of   XV, **10–19**
    transfer, e.g. conveyance, transfer, assign-
    ment.

J5 Outline the ways in which security may   XV, **10–19**
    be taken and the respective rights of bank
    and customer relating to legal and equitable
    mortgage and assignment.

Index

For a full list of titles and prices write for the
complimentary Macdonald & Evans Business Studies/
Legal Studies catalogue and/or complete M&E
Handbook list, available from Department BP1,
Macdonald & Evans Ltd., Estover Road,
Plymouth PL6 7PZ

Cases in Banking Law

PHILIP A. GHEERBRANT, *revised by* DAVID PALFREMAN

This CASEBOOK, designed to accompany the author's HANDBOOK, *Law of Banking,* is specifically written for students preparing for the Institute of Bankers Stage II examinations. A good general knowledge of the law is assumed, yet the text is written in a clear style which will be easily understandable to the non-specialist lawyer. A short introductory chapter explains how best to use the book, which contains a selection of decisions directly relevant to bankers. These cases give both a fuller background for academic purposes and useful examples of current banking practice. Recommended by the Institute of Bankers. David Palfreman was formerly a lecturer specialising in banking law at Southgate College, London. He is currently Director of the Directed Private Study Unit, St John's College, Manchester. He is also, with John Beardshaw, co-author of the M&E Business Studies Series title *The Organisation in its Environment*.

M&E Handbook Series

Finance of Foreign Trade

D.P. WHITING

This book is designed both to give a thorough grasp of the methods of international commerce and to meet the requirements of students preparing for the professional examinations in the subject. Recommended by the British Overseas Trade Board. Suitable for BTEC National, Institute of Bankers, Institute of Freight Forwarders and Institute of Export students.

M&E Handbook Series

Law of Banking

DAVID PALFREMAN

This M&E HANDBOOK has been written for banking students taking the Institute of Bankers Stage II examination. In addition to this, it provides a comprehensive summary of banking law for practising bankers and lecturers, and for those following BTEC Higher National courses in Banking Law.

M&E Handbook Series

A Dictionary of Banking
F.E. PERRY
For this new edition of an already established work of reference the author has sought to meet the needs of branch and head office officials at all levels, especially those required to serve abroad during the course of their careers, by defining not only those terms which are commonly used in English, but also those French, German and American words and phrases prevalent in modern banking and commerce. The dictionary is up-to-date, authoritative in content, comprehensive and concisely written, and produced in a format specially designed for quick and easy consultation. As an aid to the student, a glossary of "cue" words used in examination questions is reproduced from the former Journal of the Institute of Bankers as an appendix. F.E. Perry was a former Principal of the London Training Centre of one of the UK's largest banks. "A work which should be highly useful not only to bankers, but also to students and others in contact with the banking industry in this country and other countries as well." *British Book News*

M&E Professional Dictionaries series

Elements of Banking I & II
DAVID PALFREMAN & PHILIP FORD
This book has been based on the most recent specifications prepared for the BTEC double module. It is as self-sufficient as possible in relation to other BTEC National Level Modules, and is thus able to explore fully the banking perspectives (e.g. the Bankers' Conversion Course) for which the book is also suitable. The theme of the first part is banking institutions, their role in the economy and the services that they provide, along with current banking practice. The second part concentrates on current practices and issues in banking. Each chapter begins with learning objectives and concludes with a summary, and useful self-assessment questions. David Palfreman is Director of the Directed Private Study Unit at St John's College. He has many years' experience of lecturing in Banking Law, and is a well-known M&E author. Philip Ford is Training Officer at Williams & Glyns Bank and an Associate Member of the Institute.

M&E Business Studies Series

Economics: A Student's Guide
JOHN BEARDSHAW

This major new work is designed to meet the needs of students of economics who require a wide and rigorous presentation of the subject. Presupposing no knowledge of the subject, the book has been carefully designed through its graduated approach so that it will be suitable for "A" level, BTEC National and Higher level examinations, professional examinations, and for first year degree students. While the subject matter of economics remains broadly unchanged, there are periodic shifts in emphasis in its presentation and these trends have to be kept in view in any general treatment for student use. Special attention is drawn to the international aspects of economics with particular reference to Africa and India. The author, who has had long teaching experience, has also acted as a consultant in economic affairs to business concerns, and combines theory and practice to good effect from each of those spheres. An awareness of student requirements in relation to examination syllabuses (which has been the author's first consideration) is linked in his text with a sense of the importance of bringing the student into touch with the realities of the industry, trade and commerce. The treatment covers, among many other topics, mathematical techniques, demography, markets in movement (with an appendix on computer programmes), consumption savings and investment, comprehensive studies of current economic problems, economics and welfare and the economics of underdevelopment. Each chapter ends with questions and problems to help with the development of essay technique and data response. The author is Senior Tutor in Banking Studies and Lecturer in charge of Economics at Southgate Technical College. He is also, with David Palfreman, the author of the successful M&E Business Studies title, *The Organisation in its Environment.*

Monetary Theory and Practice
J.L. HANSON, *revised by* E.W. ORCHARD

The latest revision of this successful textbook is essentially an attempt to provide an easy to understand treatment of a difficult area of economics. It is aimed at those students whose courses have large sections devoted to monetary economics and will be particularly useful to students of banking, insurance, accountancy and public finance, as well as the general reader wishing to keep in touch with current economic events. The text adopts an institutional approach and analyses those institutions which make up the UK financial system. The international monetary system is then examined against the changing institutional environment of differing exchange rate systems. To give an insight into the theory behind the monetary system, the concept of money and financial intermediation is looked at and the competing theoretical economics of Keynesianism and monetarism are examined, together with their relevance for the economic policies of governments. The final part of the book attempts to give an account of how the monetary systems in both the UK and the world have developed to their present forms. For this new edition the text has been thoroughly revised and is completely up to date, taking account of the many developments in both monetary theory and practice, national and international, in recent years. Recommended by the Institute of Cost and Management Accountants. The author, J.L. Hanson, was Senior Lecturer in charge of Economics at the Huddersfield Polytechnic and has written numerous other successful textbooks on economics and commerce. The reviser, E.W. Orchard, is Senior Lecturer in Economics in the Department of Management and Business Studies at the Bolton Institute of Higher Education.

Practice of Banking I
J.E. KELLY

This important new book, which has the recommendation of the Institute of Bankers and which has been written by the present Chief Examiner in the subject, deals with topics among the most interesting and challenging in the syllabus for the aspiring banker and student. The aim is to build on the knowledge acquired in the Law Relating to Banking and for the candidate to demonstrate a firm understanding of those principles which have fashioned banking procedures over the years. Yet it is also a practical and up-to-date text guiding the student as to how a banker should act in varied situations in his or her own branch: it is therefore very relevant to any banker's daily work. Throughout the book, the author has attempted to keep the student reader and young trainee banker in mind seeking to amplify those points which, from experience, are known to prove difficult to understand, and to place emphasis on what is actually done within a branch bank. It is therefore a book not only for the examinee but also for newcomers into the profession and especially for practising security clerks and officers. The text is linked by the use of footnotes to recent questions in the Institute of Bankers' Papers, thus enabling technical points to be illustrated by the hypothetical situations posed in the examination room. J.E. Kelly is Chief Examiner for the Institute of Bankers in Practice of Banking 1 and Manager of the Securities and Recoveries Department of the National Westminster Bank plc.

Practice of Banking 2
D.G. WILD & J.R. MARSH

This book has been written specifically to meet the needs of the Institute of Bankers examination Practice of Banking 2. It will also prove useful for the practising banker as an up to date survey of advances to customers and the marketing and selling of financial services. Throughout the text emphasis is placed on practical clearing bank domestic lending situations. It is assumed in the book that some knowledge of accountancy is held. Donald Wild is Manager, Research and Development Section, Domestic Banking Division, National Westminster Bank. He also teaches practice of banking to Institute of Bankers diploma students. John Marsh is a Branch Manager with Lloyds Bank and Examiner in Marketing for the Financial Studies Diploma. Both are Fellows of the Institute of Bankers.

Sheldon and Fidler's Practice and Law of Banking
P.J.M. FIDLER

Among the significant changes in the banking world covered by this volume are the expansion of the system of supervision of banks by the Bank of England following the crisis of 1973/74 and the introduction of controls over deposit-taking institutions under the Banking Act 1979. The book now opens with an outline of the UK banking system covering these changes and includes a number of new chapters on subjects of great and growing importance to bankers in this country, such as dealing in foreign exchange, raising money on the stock exchange, underwriting and the syndication of loans, factoring, leasing and hire-purchase.

The author is a partner in a London firm of solicitors. In the course of compiling the new edition he was helped by experts from the Bank of England, the clearing banks, the merchant banks and other financial institutions.